THE LITERARY APPRECIATION
OF
RUSSIAN WRITERS

Tom Stableford

CAMBRIDGE UNIVERSITY PRESS

Cambridge

London   New York   New Rochelle

Melbourne   Sydney

Published by the Press Syndicate of the University of Cambridge
The Pitt Building, Trumpington Street, Cambridge CB2 1RP
32 East 57th Street, New York, NY 10022, USA
296 Beaconsfield Parade, Middle Park, Melbourne 3206, Australia

First published 1981

Printed in Great Britain
at the University Press, Cambridge

Library of Congress card number: 81-6192

British Library Cataloguing in Publication Data

The literary appreciation of Russian writers.
1. Russian literature
I. Stableford, T.
891.708   PG3201

ISBN 0 521 23498 0 hard covers
0 521 28003 6 paperback

THE LITERARY APPRECIATION
OF
RUSSIAN WRITERS

CONTENTS

CONTENTS

PREFACE

This book is intended to serve two purposes. One is simply to provide a basic text-book of the kind already published dealing with the literatures of the major European languages (q.v. infra). As such it will both exemplify and assist in the appreciation of literary texts in Russian. Having had the opportunity to do this kind of work with my own students, I thought it useful to collate and generalise my own experience to assist others called upon or wishing to engage in similar work. Consequently, in simple, this book is designed for Sixth-formers and undergraduates who are required to explicate Russian literary texts.

The other purpose is the broader one of promoting an awareness of the wealth of Russian literature over approximately the last two hundred years. Effectively, only a few major writers are widely known outside the Soviet Union, yet, as close readings show, there are and have been many very talented writers. Mere translation is not enough to convey a fine sensibility, hence the need to promote Russian literature through explication.

This dual purpose explains the organisation of the book. The first part contains a number of explicated passages of poetry and prose, intended not only to serve as possible models for students but also to encourage a deeper, closer reading by anyone with any knowledge at all of Russian. In order to assist the reader with only a basic knowledge of Russian, a translation (perforce fairly literal) of each text is provided. A good dictionary is of course a sine qua non, so details of several have been included in the bibliography appended below.

The second part, consisting of a number of texts of increasing length for explication (both poetry and prose), is the 'text-book' proper. Each passage is followed by a number of questions concerning theme, tone, structure, imagery, rhythm, phraseology, sound pattern, et al. These questions may be used as pointers towards a full explication or completely ignored, according to individual approach. Linguistic details will be clarified where appropriate. The author of each passage is provided to encourage further reading. Apologies are extended to those whose favourite author has been omitted but, in choosing, one is confronted with a veritable *embarras de richesses*. To assist in the task of appreciation a brief bibliography is provided below, listing a number of books either dealing with style and explication in general or providing examples of explication in the better-known European languages.

Broome, P. & Chesters, G. *The Appreciation of Modern French Poetry 1850–1950*, Cambridge, 1976.

Burnshaw, S. *The Poem Itself*, Harmondsworth, 1960.

Burton, S. H. *The Criticism of Poetry*, London, 1975.
The Criticism of Prose, London, 1975.

Carpovich, V. V. *Трудные слова у Солженицына*, Technical Dictionaries, New York, 1976.

Flegon Press, *За пределами русских словарей*, London, 1979.

Galler, M. & Marquess, H. E. *Soviet Prison Camp Speech*, Madison, Wisconsin, 1972.

Gray, R. *German Poetry: a Guide to Free Appreciation*, Cambridge, 1976.

Howarth, W. D. & Walton, C. L. *French Literary Appreciation: The Technique of 'Explications'*, Oxford, 1971.

Миртов, А. В. *Донской словарь*, Leipzig, 1971.

Ожегов, С. И. *Словарь русского языка*, Москва, 1976.

Rawlinson, D. H. *The Practice of Criticism*, Cambridge, 1960.

Thompson, E. M. *Russian Formalism and Anglo-American New Criticism*, Paris, 1971.

Unbegaun, B. O. *Russian Versification*, Oxford, 1955.

Васильева, А. Н. *Пособие для чтения со стилистическим комментарием*, Москва, 1974.

Ward, P. *Spanish Literary Appreciation*, London, 1969.

Wetherill, P. M. *The Literary Text: an Examination of Critical Methods*, London, 1974.

Wheeler, M. *The Oxford Russian–English Dictionary*, Oxford, 1972.

ACKNOWLEDGEMENTS

I would like to thank my wife, Pat, for the many hours she has spent helping me prepare this book for publication, Brian Hulme for a preliminary reading, the Governors of Manchester High School for Girls for granting me sabbatical leave to finish it, and the girls themselves without whom the book would not exist at all.

A NOTE ON SOURCES

With certain exceptions (which are listed below), the texts brought together here are taken from the standard Soviet editions of the work or writer in question.

The poem by Mandel'shtam is from vol. 1 of the collection of his writings published by Interlanguage Literary Associates Inc., Washington, D.C., 1967; the passage from a story by Yuri Kazakov is from his *Selected Short Stories*, Pergamon Press, Oxford, 1963; the passage from Solzhenitsyn's *Odin den' Ivana Denisovicha* is taken from the edition published by Possev, Frankfurt a.-M., 1966; the extract from A. H. Ostrovskiy's *Groza* is from the edition published by Bradda Books Ltd, Letchworth, Herts, 1965; the poem by Gumilyov comes from the *Sobraniye sochineniy* published by Victor Kramkin Inc., Washington D.C., 1964; Remizov's *Podstrizhennymi glazami* was published by YMCA Press, Paris, 1951; the extract from Rozanov's *Legenda o Velikom Inkvizitore: Dve stat'i o Gogole* is from the edition reprinted by W. Fink Verlag, Munich, 1970; Korzhzvin's poem is from *Vremena*, Possev, Frankfurt a.-M., 1976; the extract from 'Pkentz' by Sinyavsky-Terts is from *Fantasticheskiy mir Abrama*

Tertsa, Interlanguage Literary Associates Inc., Washington D.C., 1967; I. Brodsky's poem comes from his *Stikhotvoreniya i poemy*, Interlanguage Literary Associates Inc., Washington D.C., 1965; V. S. Grossman's *Vsyo techot* was published by Possev, Frankfurt a.-M., 1970; the edition of Zamyatin's *My* used here was published by Interlanguage Literary Associates Inc., Washington D.C., 1967; A. A. Zinov'ev's *Ziyayushchiye vysoty* was published by l'Age d'Homme, Lausanne, 1976.

PART I

Explicated Passages

АЛЕКСА́НДР СЕРГЕ́ЕВИЧ ПУ́ШКИН

(1799–1837)

Despite a more qualified reception outside the Soviet Union, Pushkin is considered there the fountain-head of all Russian literature, on a par with the world's greatest writers.

His liberal, rationalist education, begun at home and continued in Alexander I's Lycée at Tsarskoe Selo (now Pushkin), eventually brought him into contact with the pre-Decembrist political societies with which he sympathised, but which he never joined. His mildly 'revolutionary' poems caused him to be exiled in 1820 to the South. While there he wrote *Кавка́зский пле́нник*, *Бахчисара́йский Фонта́н*, most of *Цыга́ны* and the beginning of *Евге́ний Оне́гин*.

In 1824 he was ordered to stay, under police surveillance, at his parents' estate at Mikhaylovskoe in N. W. Russia. The two years spent there proved very fruitful: he wrote a great deal of lyric poetry, the play, *Бори́с Годуно́в*, finished *Цыга́ны* and continued with *Евге́ний Оне́гин*. In September 1826 the new tsar Nicholas I released him from exile, but undertook himself to be his censor. Until 1830 Pushkin wandered restlessly between Moscow and St Petersburg, producing only one major work, *Полта́ва*, in 1829. During the so-called 'Бо́лдинская о́сень' of 1830, which he spent at his parents' other estate of Boldino, he experienced a highly creative period, finishing *Евге́ний Оне́гин* and producing *До́мик в Коло́мне*, *Ма́ленькие траге́дии* and his first prose works, *По́вести Бе́лкина*.

In 1831 he married the society beauty Natal'ya Goncharova. For the rest of his life he was troubled by debts, his wife's disreputable behaviour and the tsar's interference in his work. He was unable to write much except during another sojourn at Boldino in late 1833, when he produced *Ме́дный вса́дник*. In January 1837 he was mortally wounded in a duel with a French Royalist officer in the Russian Service, Baron Georges

D'Anthès, provoked by the latter's attentions to Natal'ya. His other main prose works, *Капита́нская до́чка* and *Пи́ковая да́ма*, date from this period.

Whether he can be put on a par with the great writers from other cultures is a moot point, but he was undoubtedly outstanding in his time, completely transcending in range and versatility the narrowness of his predecessors, especially in demonstrating the unexploited scope and richness of the Russian language.

Медный всадник

(1833)

Прошло сто лет, и юный град,
Полно́щных стран краса и диво,
Из тьмы лесов, из топи блат
Вознёсся пышно, горделиво;
5.   Где прежде финский рыболов,
Печальный пасынок природы,
Один у низких берегов
Бросал в неведомые воды
Свой ветхий невод, ныне там
10.   По оживлённым берегам
Громады стройные теснятся
Дворцов и башен; корабли
Толпой со всех концов земли
К богатым пристаням стремятся;
15.   В гранит оделася Нева;
Мосты повисли над водами;
Темно-зелёными садами
Её покрылись острова,
И перед младшею столицей
20.   Померкла старая Москва,
Как перед новою царицей
Порфироносная вдова.

Люблю тебя, Петра творенье,
Люблю твой строгий, стройный вид,

25.   Невы державное теченье,
Береговой её гранит,
Твоих оград узор чугунный,
Твоих задумчивых ночей
Прозрачный сумрак, блеск безлунный,
30.   Когда я в комнате моей
Пишу, читаю без лампады,
И ясны спящие громады
Пустынных улиц, и светла
Адмиралтейская игла,
35.   И, не пуская тьму ночную
На золотые небеса,
Одна заря сменить другую
Спешит, дав ночи полчаса.

A hundred years have passed, and the youthful city,
The ornament and marvel of the boreal lands,
Has risen, proud and splendid,
From forest gloom and swampy slough;
Where once the Finnish fisherman,
Nature's sad stepson,
Sitting alone by low-lying river-banks,
Would cast his decrepit net
Into unknown waters, shapely towers and palaces
Crowd now along the busy banks;
From all corners of the world fleets of ships
Speed to its wealthy wharfs;
The Neva is clad in granite;
Bridges overhang the waters;
Its islands are bedecked
By dark-green gardens,
And beside the younger capital
Old Moscow pales,
As does a dowager queen in her purple robes
Beside a new queen.

I love you, creation of Peter,
I love your austere, shapely aspect,
The Neva's mighty flow,
Its granite embankments,

The wrought-iron tracery of your railings,
The limpid twilight and moonless brightness
Of your pensive nights,
When, without a lamp on in my room,
I can read and write,
And the sleeping bulks
Of deserted streets are still distinct,
And the Admiralty spire is bright,
And without letting nocturnal gloom
Dim the golden skies, dawn
Hastens to follow sunset,
Granting a half-hour night.

This excerpt from Pushkin's narrative poem, *Ме́дный вса́дник*, a profound treatment of the relationship between individual and society, depicts the splendour of St Petersburg a century after its founding by Peter I, and contains the famous lyrical digression by the author conveying his great love for the city. Whereas the digression is written in a tone of intimate affection, signalled by the first person narrative and the detail selected, the first half of the excerpt has the stately tone and language of an eighteenth-century ode. Consequently, the excerpt as a whole is best studied as two contrasting parts showing Pushkin's range and command of language.

Structurally, the first part operates by contrast, viz. the *пре́жде* of l.5 and *ны́не* of l.9, the primeval poverty of a Finnish swamp contrasting markedly with the cosmopolitan grandeur of the new city. The second part, a syntactical *tour de force*, is a Homeric enumeration of what endears the city to the poet. Metrically, the whole excerpt is written in Pushkin's favourite line, the iambic tetrameter with a feminine end-rhyme at the end of alternate lines. Similarly, the whole piece maintains a strict rhyme scheme of independent quatrains, but within this framework considerable variety is achieved. Furthermore, its rhythmic vitality imparts a definite élan, a readability. Regardless of tonal differences both sections are dense with images of various aspects of the city, from the *грома́ды стро́йные* of l.11 to the *лампа́да* of l.31. Although entirely visual and concrete the language of the two parts is, appropriately, different. The first half is made redolent of the eighteenth-century ode with such archaisms as *град*; *краса*; *блато*; *полнощный* and the periphrasis, *печальный пасынок природы*, while the second achieves immediacy with its use of the first person, precise detail and homely words like *комната* and *лампада*.

A 'word-count' of this extract is tedious yet revealing. Nouns, adjectives, verbs and adverbs are in proportion to each other as 11:6:3:1. Thus it is a poetry dominated by nouns and adjectives, reflecting its highly visual though static nature: the 'Northern Venice' is given real substance, very different from the insubstantial city of Gogol', Bely (q.v.) and Mandel'shtam. Consequently, the relatively small number of verbs and adverbs achieves sudden prominence amid the clustered nouns and adjectives, e.g. *теснятся* (l.11) and *стремятся* (l.14) impart considerable vigour to their lines. Phraseologically, this excerpt shows Pushkin's debt to the eighteenth century, the most obvious instance being the periphrastic *печальный пасынок природы* (l.6), but attention should be drawn to such conventional combinations as *тьма лесов* (l.3); *топь блат* (l.3); *неведомые воды* (l.8); *ветхий невод* (l.9); *стройные громады* (l.11); *державное теченье* (l.25); *тьма ночная* (l.35).

In the first line the marked caesura after *лет* draws immediate attention to the new situation, while the placing and stylistic register of *град* prepare us for the following lines. (How is one to scan *сто*?) The subsequent line, in apposition to *град* achieves a classic feeling in a number of ways: the initial archaism *полнощный* is balanced by the post-caesural *краса и диво*, itself archaic and rhetorical; inversion throws emphasis on *краса и диво*; and the consonant clusters of *полнощных стран* contrast markedly with the openness of *краса и диво*. The rhythmic ease, balance and sound (the use of *c/m/o*) of l.3 are halted in l.4, a stately, declamatory line. The verb now appears, right at the beginning of the line, demanding to be read emphatically; the comma separating the two adverbs and the suppression of the third metric stress require their being read with special emphasis. Thus, the initial quatrain, tightly encapsulated by highly appropriate rhymes (*град* is contrasted with *блат*, while *диво* is reinforced by *горделиво*) serves as a resonant introduction to the new, thriving city, presented in 17 sweeping lines.

The historical contrast touched upon in the first quatrain is now enlarged upon. Immediately the former situation is evoked by *где прежде* and the reader is carried by a complete syntactical unit through to the middle of 1.9, where the rhythmic break after *невод* and the two stressed words, *ныне там*, prepare us for early-nineteenth-century Petersburg. These same four lines form a web of subtle sound-effects: in 1.5 the interaction of the labials *п/б/в/ф* and the two *p*; the obvious alliteration of *n* in 1.6 to some extent conceals the auxiliary effect of the vowels *a* and *ы*; similarly, in 1.7 the stressed *u* and the unstressed *и/е* conceal the slight but still significant use of *н*; ll.8 and 9 can be taken as a whole sound unit – *в неведомые воды/Свой ветхий невод* – in its interweaving of vowels and consonants. The subtle change in the rhyme-scheme links *ныне там* with what follows by rhyming it with *берегам*. The remaining eleven lines of vigorous detail are cleverly encapsulated by their rhyme-scheme, especially the linking of the final *вдова* with *Москва/острова/Нева*.

How does Pushkin convey the excitement and majesty of the scene? Primarily by the whole section from *ныне там* to *вдова* being a single syntactical unit in which half a dozen clauses are packed together. Secondly, by the placing of significant words: line 10 has in reality only two metric stresses (on -*ё*- and -*ам*), thereby emphasising its vowels. Similarly, the meaning of *теснятся* is well illustrated by its placing between *громады стройные* and *дворцов и башен*. The rhythmic break after *башен* picks out *корабли* whence the line rushes to the verb *стремятся*, suspended until the end. Vowels and consonants play their part in these lines, especially *с/a*. The pace is suddenly slowed down at 1.15 which links, as mentioned above, with the last word of this section. The perfective verb *оделася* sets the picture in the present, while the absence of rhythmic/metrical counterpoint imparts an appropriate force to all three words. The two perfective verbs in ll.16 and 18 have the same effect of making the scene immediate. The rhyme-scheme *abba* links together all these details. Placing of words serves to create a picture of bridges, water, gardens and islands, through which run the sounds *c* and *a*. Finally, the faded grandeur of the old capital, Moscow, is conveyed by more than simile. Word-order is used to effect, especially the placing of *померкла* and, by inverted syntax, the last line *порфироносная вдова*, further heightened by metre/rhythm counterpoint and vowel-sounds, all utterly lost in translation.

Syntactically, the last lines are exactly balanced by the pre-positional phrase preceding the subject, while sound (*n/p/c/ц/e/o/a*) and rhyme encapsulate the whole.

A typographical break and a complete change of tone introduce the famous lyrical digression. This tonal change is effected immediately by *люблю тебя* and is maintained by the author's presence and recurrence of the familiar *твой*. The use of the formal *вы/ваш* would have had a completely different effect. This whole section is a syntactical *tour de force*, beginning with *люблю* and sweeping unbroken to *полчаса*. This and the use of few verbs enables Pushkin to give a proselike density to the picture he creates. Why are the first two lines so memorable? Primarily from the lyric immediacy of placing *люблю* at the beginning of each line, but also from syntactical directness, rhythmic firmness and the interweaving of the sounds *m/p/c/o/e*. In the subsequent five lines the frequent inversions highlight the objects selected. This dense group of nouns and adjectives (N.B. absence of verbs) takes on further meaning with the sudden introduction of the homely l.30, while the adjacent verbs point out that the main activities in his life, writing and reading, can take place at night *без лампады*, thus elucidating the unusual placing of *прозрачный* with *сумрак* in l.29 and *безлунный* with *блеск*. The main feature of the 'white nights' is highlighted by the inverted placing of the short adjectives *ясны* and *светла*, especially since *светла* receives metric and positional emphasis by standing at the end of the line. At the same time this allows a whole, striking line to the feature picked out by Mandel'shtam nearly a century later, the Admiralty spire. The third *и* at the head of l.35 leads into the final quatrain, where the verb is delayed with great effect until the last line; effective, because what is emphasised is the speed with which sunrise follows sunset (Pushkin plays cleverly upon the double meaning of *заря*). The remarkable brevity of the Petersburg summer night is pointed out by the emphatic placing of the final word *полчаса*.

НИКОЛА́Й ВАСИ́ЛЬЕВИЧ ГО́ГОЛЬ

(1809–52)

Born into a poor Ukrainian gentry family in Sorochintsy in the Poltava district, Gogol′ remained there until he completed his education in 1828, when he left for St Petersburg with hopes of a literary career in the capital. His initial weak efforts at poetry were met with scorn, so he temporarily gave up his ambition and became a government clerk. To forget his dreary life he wrote *Вечера́ на ху́торе близ Дика́ньки* in 1831–2. Unlike the poetry these were well received by many, including Pushkin. Interested in the picturesque, romantic side of history he planned, but never wrote, vast historical works. Such plans were mainly formulated during his brief and disastrous sojourn as Professor of History at St Petersburg University in 1834–5. In 1835 he wrote *Ми́ргород*, consisting of four tales, still with a Ukrainian setting, but more imaginative in scope. *Старо-све́тские поме́щики* is a gently satirical idyll; *Тара́с Бу́льба* is a historical romance; *Вий* a grim fantasy, while *По́весть о том, как поссо́рился Ива́н Ива́нович с Ива́ном Ники́форовичем* is uproariously and painfully satirical. *Арабе́ски* (1835) contains essays and stories, the latter (*Не́вский проспе́кт; Портре́т; Запи́ски сумасше́дшего*) set in St Petersburg, shown in a dream-like blend of the sordid and the fantastic. His famous comic satire on provincial bureaucracy, *Ревизо́р*, was staged in 1836.

From 1836 to 1848 he lived mostly abroad, often in Rome, whose magnificence fascinated him. In 1842 were published his satirical masterpiece, *Мёртвые ду́ши* (Part 1), his best-known short story, *Шине́ль*, and the comedy, *Жени́тьба*.

Gogol′ was deeply conscious of his moral responsibility as a writer, and his satires on bureaucracy and serfdom were inter-preted by contemporary radicals (and Soviet critics) as blows in the struggle for progress. Yet for Gogol′ himself it was moral, rather than social or political evil he was castigating. In fact, he saw the former as real, embodied forces in the world. He continually brooded over his feelings of guilt and insufficiency, and the roots of all his satire lie in his complex personality, riddled with anxieties and obsessions. He laboured vainly over the second part of *Мёртвые ду́ши* which was to show the transformation and regeneration of its negative characters, but burnt the manuscript. In 1847 he published *Вы́бранные места́ из перепи́ски с друзья́ми*, a collection of moralising essays defending Tsarism in the spirit of conservative, religious orthodoxy, for which he was labelled *апостол кнута* by Belinsky. In his last years he became a prey to despair and religious mania and ceased writing.

Повесть о том, как поссорился Иван Иванович с Иваном Никифоровичем

(1835)

Тощая баба выносила по порядку залежалое платье и развешивала его на протянутой верёвке выветривать. Скоро старый мундир с изношенными обшлагами протянул на воздух рукава и обнимал парчовую кофту; за ним высунулся дворянский, и с гербовыми пуговицами, с отъеденным воротником; белые казимировые панталоны с пятнами, которые когда-то натягивались на ноги Ивана Никифоровича и которые можно теперь натянуть разве на его пальцы. За ними скоро повисли другие в виде буквы Л. Потом синий козацкий бешмет, который шил себе Иван Никифорович назад тому лет двадцать, когда готовился вступить в милицию и отпустил было уже усы. Наконец, одно к одному, выставилась шпага, походившая на шпиц, торчавший в воздухе. Потом завертелись фалды чего-то похожего на кафтан травяно-зелёного цвета, с медными пуговицами величиною в пятак. Из-за фалд выглянул жилет, обложенный золотым позументом с большим вырезом напереди.

Жилет скоро закрыла старая юбка покойной бабушки, с карманами, в которые можно было положить по арбузу. Всё, мешаясь вместе, составляло для Ивана Ивановича очень занимательное зрелище, между тем как лучи солнца, охватывая местами синий или зелёный рукав, красный обшлаг или часть золотой парчи, или играя на шпажном шпице, делали его чем-то необыкновенным, похожем на тот вертеп, который развозят по хуторам кочующие пройдохи. Особливо, когда толпа народа, тесно сдвинувшись, глядит на царя Ирода в золотой короне или на Антона, ведущего козу; за вертепом визжит скрипка; цыган бренчит руками по губам своим вместо барабана, а солнце заходит, и свежий холод южной ночи незаметно прижимается сильнее к свежим плечам и грудям полных хуторянок.

Next the skinny woman brought out a long unused dress and hung it on a clothes-line to air. An old dress-coat with thread-bare cuffs had soon stretched its sleeves into the air and was embracing a brocade jacket; after it a dress-coat with a moth-eaten collar and buttons bearing the family crest thrust itself forward; with it were white cashmere trousers covered in stains which were once pulled onto Ivan Nikiforovich's legs but now would scarcely fit his fingers. After them another pair, in the shape of a Russian L, were soon hanging out. Then came a dark-blue Cossack quilted coat which Ivan Nikiforovich had had made some twenty years ago when he was preparing to join the police force and on the point of growing a moustache. Finally a sword, looking like a spire sticking up in the air, was brought out as well. Then fluttered the skirts of something looking like a grass-green kaftan with enormous brass buttons. From behind the skirts peeped a gold-braided waistcoat with a low neck.

The waistcoat was soon covered by his late grandmother's old skirt with pockets into which you could put a whole water-melon. All of this mixing together provided Ivan Ivanovich with a very entertaining spectacle while the sun's rays, in clasping here and there a dark-blue or green sleeve, a red cuff or a piece of gold brocade, made it something extra-ordinary, like the Nativity play taken round the villages by wandering scoundrels. Especially when the closely packed crowd stares at King Herod's gold crown or at Anton leading his goat; behind it squeaks the fiddle and a gipsy strums on his lips in place of a drum as the sun goes down and the fresh cold southern night presses unnoticeably more and more on the fresh shoulders and breasts of plump village girls.

This extensive descriptive passage is basically a description of a line of washing, but is transformed into a memorable event by

Gogol''s unique imaginative powers. A humour, often degenerating into the grotesque, pervades and directs the piece. Its effectiveness is partly the result of its simple but skilful structure. The device of the washing-line allows Gogol' to compile, sentence by sentence, an inventory of some of the other Ivan's dress, including his sword. Yet he is not content with a mere list. All these elements are combined and re-deployed by the sentence beginning *всё, мешаясь вместе* ... At this point tricks of sunlight suggest to Gogol' a travelling Ukrainian puppet theatre, and thus a structural climax is reached with an extensive Homeric simile. As so often in Gogol''s work a relatively ordinary scene is transformed into something very different, as inanimate objects take on a life of their own.

If Chekhov stands at one end of the range of Russian prose styles in his spareness, Gogol' could be placed at the other in his baroque splendour with, to pursue the metaphor, all the excesses of that style. The images of Gogol''s world are a great concatenation of objects, many very strange; blending with these objects are scarcely distinguished sub-human beings. The range of his vocabulary is enormous and one inevitably requires the assistance of a dictionary – this passage is no exception. Its visual impact is tremendous, the result of the author's using an essentially concrete but highly elaborate, sometimes unusual, vocabulary. Yet in the great array of substantives in this excerpt, ranging from those as stylistically neutral as *пальцы*; *ноги*, to those with a Ukrainian colouring, such as *вертеп*; *хуторянка*, few stand alone: adjectives are used with almost equal frequency, especially those describing a colour – the washing-line is a grotesque rainbow (when not transformed into a travelling puppet-theatre). In fact, almost every noun is qualified. Gogol' has relatively little recourse to adverbs except those with a structural function (*скоро* is employed three times, along with *теперь*; *потом*; *наконец*), since his use of verbs imparts such vigour to the scene, e.g. *протянул*; *натянуть*; *высунулся*; *играя*; *визжит*; *бренчит*.

However, it is the idiosyncratic association of nouns, adjectives and verbs which sets Gogol' in the world of Sterne, Dickens and Peake. There is nothing splendid about the washing of this ostensibly splendid Ivan, e.g. *залежалое платье*; *старый мундир с изношенными обшлагами; с отъеденным воротником; панталоны с пятнами*, yet Gogol' imparts a brilliance to this ragged array with his use of epithets of colour, viz. *белый; синий; травяно-зелёный; золотой; красный*, some of which are repeated. Especially notable is his animation of the inanimate (and the opposite, elsewhere in this and other works) e.g. *мундир ... протянул ... рукава и обнимал парчовую кофту; высунулся дворянский; из-за фалд выглянул жилет; жилет скоро закрыла старая юбка; лучи солнца, охватывая ... играя; и свежий холод ... прижимается*. Above all, it is the sudden entrance of the absurd or grotesque that identifies Gogol''s style; the entrance of a unique and striking phraseology, e.g. *белые казимировые панталоны с пятнами, которые когда-то натягивались на ноги Ивана Никифоровича и которые можно теперь натянуть разве на его пальцы; другие в виде буквы Л; с медными пуговицами величиною в пятак; с карманами, в которые можно было положить по арбузу.*

All these features together impart a very noticeable rhythm to the passage, the essence of which lies in Gogol''s often very extensive qualification of the substantives describing observed objects or actions, and his scarcely controlled infatuation with them. The short, terse sentence is a rarity. Much of the effect of Gogol''s prose on the reader is the result of its great rhythmic surges, one after the other, building up to a climax. Thus, the first two sentences are lengthened by being, in fact, four clauses; moreover, in each, either the grammatical subject or object (or both) is extended, i.e. *старый мундир с изношенными обшлагами*. Then follows *дворянский, с гербовыми пуговицами, с отъеденным воротником* and, presumably referring to *высунулся*, the remarkable *белые казимировые панталоны с пятнами, которые когда-то натягивались на ноги Ивана Никифоровича и которые можно теперь натянуть разве на его пальцы*, separated only by a semi-colon. A brief ebb before *Потом синий козацкий бешмет, который шил себе Иван Никифорович назад тому лет двадцать, когда готовился вступить в милицию и отпустил было уже усы.* Thus it continues until one is given respite with the climactic *всё*. The power of these surges is rendered greater by the unobtrusive but effective employment of adverbs, i.e. *по порядку ... скоро ... за ним ... за ними ... потом ... наконец ... потом*. After *всё*, the impact of the simile (appropriately an extended, Homeric one) is heightened by a renewed rhythmic surge which sweeps all the way down to *пройдохи*. This is achieved by multiple subordination of clauses and the extension of substantives. If one ignores the semi-colons, the passage sweeps rapidly from *особливо* to the final *хуторянок*. Yet again the same observations apply, although there is greater vigour in the scene because of the relative proximity of the verbs *глядит* ... *визжит* ... *бренчит* ... *заходит* ... *прижимается*.

On examining this and many other similar passages closely, one is soon led to ask what the precise significance of such verbal luxury is. To what extent does it advance the plot? To what extent does it provide further details about the lives and characters of the two Ivans? The answer to both is generally – very little. In reality, a close study of this and other passages by Gogol' shows an apparently uncontrolled delight in language and its employment to create a world teeming with objects. Each sentence shows his concern to say something, very often negative, about each object: the *баба* (not *старуха* or *женщина*) is *тощая*, the *платье* is *залежалое*, the *мундир* is not simply *старый* but *с изношенными обшлагами*. This is carried to a grotesque degree when we are told about the *панталоны* and the *юбка*. One is often at a loss to know why certain information is imparted, especially *Потом синий козацкий бешмет, который шил себе Иван Никифорович назад тому лет двадцать, когда готовился вступить в милицию и отпустил было уже усы.* As noted above, this may be a grotesque world, but it is not a dull one – bright colours abound from first to last.

Though contributing to a rhythmic *tour de force* the long simile is not a precise one, sharpening our vision of the object being compared. It is, rather, an expression of Gogol''s vision of the world, where objects are suddenly and strangely transformed. It not only comprises the puppets of the 'vertep', but also its sounds (absent from the washing-line), the villagers and the Ukrainian climate. In this and his other works Gogol' never deals with women as ordinary human beings – they are either idealised or reduced, like his male characters, to grotesque dolls (e.g. Agaf'ya Fedos'evna in this tale). Hence the conventional triteness of the last line with its *свежие* and *полные*. All these effects are heightened still further by a subtle sound pattern pervading the passage, changing with each rhythmic group, e.g. the sounds к/л/н/т/о/а in *белые казимировые панталоны с пятнами, которые когда-то натягивались на ноги Ивана Никифоровича и которые можно теперь натянуть разве на его пальцы,* or the sounds *б/р/м/а* in *цыган бренчит руками по губам своим вместо барабана.*

ФЁДОР ИВА́НОВИЧ ТЮТЧЕВ

(1803–73)

Tyutchev was born into an old nobility family in the village of Ovstug in Bryansk province in 1803. Receiving a good education at home from his tutor, the poet Raich, he began creative writing early: he had a version of the poetry of Horace published in 1819. From 1819 to 1821 he studied in the literature faculty of Moscow University. After leaving university in 1822 he enrolled in the Foreign Ministry which entailed his serving at the Russian Diplomatic Mission in Munich until 1837 and in Turin from 1837 to 1839. While in Munich he married a Bavarian noblewoman and during this time, also, his poetry and translations of such authors as Heine were published in Moscow literary journals. In 1836 Pushkin, very impressed by Tyutchev's poetry, published a selection in the literary magazine, *Современник*. On his return to Russia in 1844 Tyutchev remained in government service, occupying from 1848 the ministerial post of Senior Censor, and from 1858 to the end of his life he headed the Committee for the Censorship of Foreign Literature.

Tyutchev was formed as a mature poet in the late 1820s and early 1830s. Some of his best lyrics, including 'Silentium!', belong to this period. Typically, they are passionate, lyrical expressions of ideas and are imbued with an acute sense of the tragic in life. His second period of major creative activity came at the end of the 1840s, culminating in a highly acclaimed collection of his poetry being published in 1854. It was after this period and on into the 1860s that Tyutchev wrote his best love poetry, a poetry remarkable both in its perceptive revelation of human experiences and its mastery of unconventional rhythms.

Although liberal in his youth, with the development of revolutionary events in Europe, Tyutchev's conservative tendencies were strengthened, taking on a Pan-Slav colouring in the late 1840s, when he came to see autocratic Russia, called upon to unite all the Slav peoples, as a bastion against revolution (v. his poem, *Мóре и утёс*). His philosophical views were formed under the influence of the German Romantic philosopher Schelling, of whom he was a personal friend. In his poetry the world, Nature and Man are the scenes of a constant clash of opposing forces. Man is doomed to a 'hopeless' – *безнадёжный* – struggle with life, Fate and himself. Tyutchev was much drawn to the depiction of storms both in Nature and in the human soul. Along with Boratynsky (q.v.) he is considered the main representative of Russian 'metaphysical' lyric poetry of the nineteenth century.

'Silentium!'

(1833)

Молчи, скрывайся и таи
И чувства и мечты свои –
Пускай в душевной глубине
Встают и заходят оне
Безмолвно, как звёзды в ночи, –
Любуйся ими – и молчи.

7.   Как сердцу высказать себя?
Другому как понять тебя?
Поймёт ли он, чем ты живёшь?
Мысль изречённая есть ложь;
Взрывая, возмутишь ключи, –
Питайся ими – и молчи.

13.   Лишь жить в самом себе умей –
Есть целый мир в душе твоей
Таинственно-волшебных дум;
Их оглушит наружный шум,
Дневные разгонят лучи, –
Внимай их пенью – и молчи! . . .

Keep silent, hide yourself and conceal
Your feelings and your dreams –
In the depths of your soul
Let them rise and set,
In silence, like stars in the night –
Admire them – but keep silent.

How can the heart express itself?
How can another understand you?
Will he understand what you live by?
A thought uttered is a falsehood;
By stirring up the springs you will cloud them, –
Imbibe them – but keep silent.

Know how to live the inner life –
In your soul there is a whole world
Of mysterious, magical thoughts;
Outer noise will drown them,
Daylight will drive them away, –
Heed their singing – but keep silent! . . .

This brief, well-known poem expresses the typically Romantic view that one's deepest thoughts and feelings can never be adequately expressed; that since they perforce are distorted by reality, they are best left unsaid. The terse classical title betrays the influence of the only two poets whose influence Tyutchev recognised, viz. Derzhavin and Lomonosov, on the tone of the poem in its lofty, hortatory (it contains eleven imperatives) impersonality and intellectuality, weighty with abstractions and archaisms.

Part of that impact which has given this poem its enduring quality lies in its organisation, basically a triple restatement of its theme – *молчи!* – reiterated at the end of each stanza. Furthermore, the identity of the first and last words encapsulates the theme. Within this framework each stanza falls into two parts – an abstract statement and its metaphorical restatement in concrete imagery. Thus, restatement within restatement; simple, but powerful in its insistence. Turgenev noted a similar structure and development in many of Tyutchev's poems: '*Каждое его стихотворение начинается мыслью, но мыслью, которая, как огненная точка, вспыхивала под влиянием глубокого чувства или сильного впечатления.*'

Each six-line stanza is written in iambic tetrameter, the Russian 'heroic', an appropriately dignified metre for such a highly intellectual, serious poem. Yet the strength of feeling behind this 'metaphysical' poem over-rides the metre to such an extent (c.f. Donne's 'Song') that it bursts its bonds and becomes accentual verse, viz. ll.4, 5, 10 and 17. Failing to see this, Turgenev rewrote these lines as 'correct' iambics. The strict rhyme-scheme *aabbcc* both tightly controls and clinches each stanza.

Although the vocabulary of this poem is predominantly abstract, e.g. *чувства; мечты; мысль; ложь; понять; мир; дум,* these abstractions are given 'a local habitation and a name' by the concrete imagery of the metaphors, i.e. *звёзды в ночи; ключи; наружный шум; дневные ... лучи.* In fact there is a subtle mixture of the simple and the elaborate (*таинственно-волшебных; молчи*), the concrete and the abstract (*звёзды; мысль изречённая*), and the sensuous and the intellectual (*питайся ими; высказать себя*). A further dimension is added through each metaphor's appealing to a different sense, viz. visual, gustatory and aural. The large number of nouns is balanced by an almost equal number of verbs, thus the intellectual element expressed through the nouns is balanced by the emotional vigour of the verbs (half of which are imperatives). The solitary adverb *безмолвно* is thematically entirely appropriate. A limited use of adjectives imparts a certain spareness, as it were keeping the poem's content above the concrete world. When adjectives are used they are carefully chosen, and often striking, e.g. *целый; изречённая; таинственно-волшебный.* The complete absence of the first person contributes to the poem's impersonality, while the imperatives and the use of the familiar second person convey the strength of feeling.

In the first line of the poem punctuation, placing and rhythm emphasise the three verbs which fully state the theme and its implications. Yet their very isolation arouses attention and curiosity, viz. why remain silent (Tyutchev certainly did not!) and shun society? The provocative position of the transitive verb *таи* at the end of the line draws us inevitably to its object in the second line and completes the sense: one must hide one's deepest feelings and thoughts. These first two lines form a beautifully balanced couplet: the verbs form the first line, the nouns the second, each word given metric and rhythmical stress; the rhyme highlights two very important words: *таи;* *свои*, while the interweaving of the sounds *c/m/u* runs through the two lines. The visual metaphor of the next four lines both explains and augments the initial couplet. The dash after *свои* compels us to pause and heed Tyutchev's advice, while *пускай* creates suspense because it requires a verb, suspended until l.4. The weighty metaphor *в душевной глубине* dominates the line, literally and intellectually. Although not an original metaphor it is strong in context. In the following line the collapse of the metric scheme and the consequent rhythmic tension inevitably put great emphasis on the two verbs and their meaning – let one's feelings and deepest thoughts complete their course (an astronomical image) entirely within. The archaic *оне* seems a mere nonce-rhyme, but is acceptable because of the eighteenth-century 'feel' of the language as a whole. The enjambement of the only adverb in the poem, viz. *безмолвно*, inevitably gives it considerable emphasis – indeed it reiterates the theme. The image of stars is very appropriate because they, like unuttered thoughts, have a silent beauty. Lines 5 and 6 exhibit a careful and deliberate use of punctuation: the comma and the dash at the end of l.5 precede two more imperatives, themselves separated by a dash acting as a caesura. The effect is: admire your star-thoughts – in silence. The final *молчи* clinches the stanza by position, echo and rhyme.

Half of the second stanza is taken up by three impassioned rhetorical questions, justifying the dogmatic statement of the first stanza. Highly intellectual in vocabulary and content these lines exhibit Tyutchev's metric skills and ease. Word-stress and metre coincide exactly in l.7, thereby giving equal importance to each word. By end-stopping, the question is put with maximum effect. Moreover, the sibilant *c* in the three stressed words adds still more emphasis. The foregoing is also true of l.8 – in this case the metric stress on *как*, a normally unstressed word, questions the impossibility of mutual comprehension still more. The caesura in l.9 creates a strong antithesis in a single line – between the stressed *он* and *ты*. In delivery the famous tenth line is effectively accentual, putting all the emphasis on the three words with an implied caesura dividing the tremendous *мысль изречённая* (an appropriately archaic verb) from the hammer-blow of *ложь.* This is a truly 'classic' line in both form and content. Yet Tyutchev gives all this abstraction flesh through the metaphor of muddying deep, clear springs. The comma after the gerund compels meditation on the implications of the verb. The confusion and damage conveyed by this line is given aural expression through consonant clusters. As in the first stanza a dash precedes the poet's exhortation. *Питайся ими* is pointed up by the dash acting as a caesura: let feelings and thoughts nourish you – but in silence. To emphasise the close connection, *молчи*, with its plangent stressed vowel echoes the first stanza.

In the third stanza the conclusion of l.13 on the imperative *умей* emphasises the exhortation. One is compelled to pause by the dash before proceeding to the explanation, introduced by one of Tyutchev's favourite words, *есть*, stating the existence of certain states or situations. In this case the verb is followed by the two-line sweep of a single phrase: syntax is exploited to point out the richness of this complete spiritual world by the isolation of the remarkable line *таинственно-волшебных дум* – the large number of unstressed vowels creates its rhythm, yet stress is still put on the important word *дум*. Rhyming with it is the operative word of the aural metaphor of l.16 – *шум* (notice the interplay of the sounds *ш/ж/у*). A sudden change to accentual metre and the concomitant change of rhythm pick out l.17. Yet again the dash acting as caesura attracts attention to both parts of the final line, redolent of the eighteenth century in its vocabulary. The final, emphatic *молчи!*, clinched by rhyme, echoes the very first word, thus skilfully encapsulating and reiterating.

ИВÁН СЕРГÉЕВИЧ ТУРГÉНЕВ

(1818–83)

From an Oryol gentry family, Turgenev was dominated by a tyrannical mother in his boyhood. He studied at the Universities of Moscow, St Petersburg and Berlin, returning thence in the forties a liberal and 'Westerniser'. He achieved literary fame with a series of pictures of peasant life, *Запúски охóтника* (1847–51), which supposedly influenced Alexander II in his desire to abolish serfdom.

Although he wrote some poetry, short stories and plays (the most notable being the proto-Chekhovian *Мéсяц в дерéвне* of 1850), his best and most famous work was in the novel form, especially *Рýдин* (1856), *Дворянское гнездó* (1859), *Наканýне* (1860), *Отцы́ и дéти* (1862). Disillusioned by the blinkered criticism of the latter by the Russian radicals, he effectively emigrated to Western Europe, living in Baden-Baden from 1862 to 1870 and Paris from 1871 to 1883. His last novels, *Дым* (1867) and *Новь* (1877), reflect his increasing loss of sympathy for the radical elements in Russia. Awarded an honorary degree by Oxford University in 1879, a friend of Flaubert, the Goncourts and Zola, he was the first Russian writer to enjoy an international reputation. His great technical skill as a novelist and stylist was fully recognised by Henry James who called him 'the novelist's novelist'.

Накануне

(1860)

Между тем Елена вернулась в свою комнату, села перед раскрытом окном и оперлась головой на руки. Проводить каждый вечер около четверти часа у окна своей комнаты вошло у ней в привычку. Она беседовала сама с собою в это время, отдавала себе отчёт в протёкшем дне. Ей недавно минул двадцатый год. Росту она была высокого, лицо имела бледное и смуглое, большие серые глаза под круглыми бровями, окружённые крошечными веснушками, лоб и нос совершенно прямые, сжатый рот и довольно острый подбородок. Её темно-русая коса спускалась низко на тонкую шею. Во всём её существе, в выражении лица, внимательном и немного пугливом, в ясном, но изменчивом взоре, в улыбке, как будто напряжённой, в голосе, тихом и неровном, было что-то нервическое, электрическое, что-то порывистое и торопливое, словом что-то такое, что не могло всем нравиться, что даже отталкивало иных. Руки у ней были узкие, розовые с длинными пальцами, ноги тоже узкие; она ходила быстро, почти стремительно, но немного наклоняясь вперёд. Она росла очень странно; сперва обожала отца, потом страстно привязалась к матери и охладела к обоим, особенно к отцу. В последнее время она обходилась матерью, как с больною бабушкой; а отец, который гордился ею, пока она слыла за необыкновенного ребёнка, стал её бояться, когда она выросла, и говорил о ней, что она какая-то восторженная республиканка, Бог знает в кого! Слабость возмущала её, глупость сердила, ложь она не прощала ''во веки веков''; требования её ни перед чем не отступали, самые молитвы не раз мешались с укором. Стоило человеку потерять её уважение, – а суд произносила она скоро, часто слишком скоро, – и уж он переставал существовать для неё. Все впечатления резко ложились в её душу; не легко давалась ей жизнь.

Meanwhile Yelena went back to her room, sat down in front of the open window resting her head on her arms. It had become a habit of hers to spend about a quarter of an hour every evening sitting by the window of her room. It was at this time that she would talk to herself, pondering the day's events. She was just nineteen. She was tall with a pallid yet dark complexion, big grey eyes beneath curved brows and surrounded by tiny freckles, a perfectly straight forehead and nose, a tight mouth and a rather pointed chin. Her brown pigtail came low down on her slender neck. There was something nervous and electric, something jerky and hurried about her whole being, about her attentive and slightly timid expression, about her clear but changeable gaze, about her somehow tense smile and about her quiet, uneven voice; in a word, something not to everyone's taste, even repellent to some. Her pink, long-fingered hands were narrow, as were her legs; she walked quickly, almost impetuously, leaning forward slightly. She had developed very strangely; at first she had adored her father, then became passionately attached to her mother, then became cool to both, especially her father. Recently she had been treating her mother like an invalid grandmother; her father, proud of her when she was thought of as an unusual child, began to be afraid of her when she had grown up, saying of her that she was an enthusiastic republican of some sort, the Lord knows whom she takes after! Weakness made her indignant, stupidity angered her, lying she would never, ever forgive; she made no concessions, even her prayers contained reproach. One only had to lose her respect – and judgement was quickly pronounced, often too quickly – and that person absolutely ceased to exist for her. All impressions made a harsh mark on her; life was not easy for her.

In this detailed physical and psychological description of Yelena, the heroine of *Накануне*, the tone of Turgenev's omniscient narrative is somewhat aloof and slightly critical – she has an unpleasant effect on some people, her psychological development has been very strange, her judgements on people too hasty, etc. This portrait is conveyed by a very skilfully and carefully constructed piece of prose. The passage falls into three parts: the section *Между тем . . . дне* allows the reader to observe and picture her; a detailed physical description is provided by the section *Ей . . . вперёд*, and from there to the end an insight is given into her mental life. In the latter two main sections particular details lead to general conclusions, although the first half of the second section does develop from a general statement about her. These 'sections' are not, however, disconnected, since the latter to some extent explains the former, thus creating a unified, composite picture within the framework of a single paragraph.

Compared with Gogol''s (q.v.) this is strikingly 'plain' prose, eschewing figurative imagery, but employing structure and vocabulary to the maximum extent. This vocabulary belongs to what might be called the 'middle' register – apart from a few words denoting intellectual or emotional concepts, e.g. *слабость; глупость; ложь; уважение*, the vocabulary is concrete and literal. Moreover, there is a varied and subtle deployment of parts of speech: the first part is predominantly nouns and adjectives, occasionally qualified by adverbs, the resultant portrait being a static one; the second part, dominated by verbs, is more dynamic and therefore appropriate to convey Yelena's psychological and emotional development. In this section adverbs are used much more vigorously, strengthening verbs. As will be seen, this neither striking nor idiosyncratic use of language achieves great effect through syntax and rhythm.

Half a dozen paratactic clauses create the basis for the ensuing description. By employing the imperfective aspect Turgenev is showing Yelena in a typical pose, intimating also something of her intellectual attitudes in her questioning of each day's events: she does not simply 'live' her life, she feels a need to understand it. This introductory and extensive parataxis gives a clipped, diaristic rhythm and thereby quickly sets the scene. The very brief reference to her age serves to point out that she is between adolescence and maturity, thus, although the more brittle aspects of her personality may be outgrown, other features will almost certainly remain with her.

The long sentence devoted to her physical features operates by accumulation of detail through a series of nouns and adjectives, using only two stylistically neutral verbs. The parallelism of *росту* and *лицо* highlights these features. Further on, subtle changes in word-order provide rhythmic and syntactic variety: *большие серые глаза; лоб и нос совершенно прямые; сжатый рот.* Co-ordination is limited to *и*, thus continuing the parataxis of the initial section. Because of the commas the effect of such syntax is to make each detail precise, like jigsaw pieces. The reference to *коса* in the following isolated sentence captures the attention – does she wish to identify with the Russian people through the wearing of a pigtail, although physically she is not one of them? (N.B. the deliberate reference to her *тонкую шею.*) After this series of brief telegraphic phrases the long sentence *во всём ... отталкивало иных* is logically, syntactically and rhythmically climactic. *Во всём её существе,* placed at the beginning, serves to state that the ensuing sums up her physical effect on others. This is heightened by the syntactic parallelism of a series of prepositional phrases and the concomitant rhythm of accumulation; the subject of *было* operates with a similar parallelism and rhythmic accumulation, thus creating a secondary parallelism of predicate and subject.

The telling use of adjectives and adverbs, again virtually in parallel, heightens the effect of her slightly unusual, disarming physical appearance. The triple use of an indefinite pronoun, the strikingly modern (in context) *нервическое и электрическое* and the unattractive *порывистое и торопливое* justify the following comments on her effect on some people.

The reference to her long, thin hands and legs serves to make the transition to the psychological dimension by reference to her gait, again unusual: *почти стремительно, но немного наклоняясь вперёд*. Her unusual personality is immediately pointed out by the provocative and curt *Она росла очень странно*. In the ensuing, verbs and adverbs dynamically convey the strength of the several sudden changes in her feelings: *обожала ... страстно привязалась ... охладела ... обходила ... как с больною бабушкой*. As above, the impact of this is increased by its telegraphic rhythm. Her father's changing feelings are also conveyed by verbs, viz. *гордился ... стал её бояться* and the carefully chosen, slightly ironic *какая-то*, intimating his incomprehension. At this point there is a sudden change of syntax – the rhythm of multiple hypotaxis (the only occasion in this piece) encapsulates the changes in, and confusion of, his attitudes. The strength of her intellect is vividly conveyed by parallel inversion of object and subject, the use of strong verbs: *возмущала ... сердила ... не прощала*, and a paratactic rhythm. Emphasis is achieved in the following two short clauses not by syntax but rather by choice of words, viz. *требования её ни перед чем не отступали, самые молитвы не раз мешались с укором*. The rashness of her judgements finds its expression in the subtle use of the dash, causing the reader to pause to consider the process described. The harshness of such judgements is well conveyed by the strong phrase *переставал существовать*. A partial justification is contained in the deliberately chosen *резко*. The final brief sentence is a great understatement; in these few words so much is said about Yelena at nineteen and her place in the world.

М. Ю. ЛÉРМОНТОВ

(1814–41)

Born in Moscow, he was transferred to his grandmother's estate at the age of three on the death of his mother, leaving behind his father, a retired officer of Scottish extraction. He was educated at home and paid three visits to the Caucasus while still young. He studied at Moscow University from 1830 to 1832, but did not take any examinations. Straight after this he entered the Petersburg Guards' Cadet School where he wrote both bawdy and lyrical verse, including the famous *Белéет пáрус одинóкий*.

As an officer in the Guards' Hussars (1834) and in society-life he became increasingly cynical. He was arrested on Pushkin's death in 1837 for an anti-autocratic poem, expelled from the Guards and sent to the Army in the Caucasus. On his return to Moscow he became involved in a duel in 1840 and was again banished to the Caucasus just as his novel, *Герóй нáшего врéмени*, was published. He was killed in a senseless duel in 1841.

He was an embittered romantic in both life and literature, fascinated by Napoleon and, above all, Byron, whom he imitated in life and literature, though realising his own identity to be Russian and therefore ultimately different. His work is full of typically romantic themes and images, but his orientalism is inspired by the Caucasus. His poetry replaces a diary or correspondence as a confessional device in which he reveals his aspirations, conflict with and revolt against society. Towards the end of his life he turned away from romantic themes, but any further development was cut short by an untimely death.

Тучи

(1840)

Тучки небесные, вечные странники!
Степью лазурною, цепью жемчужною
Мчитесь вы, будто как я же, изгнанники,
С милого севера в сторону южную.

5. Кто же вас гонит: судьбы ли решение?
Зависть ли тайная, злоба-ль открытая?
Или на вас тяготит преступление,
Или друзей клевета ядовитая?
Нет, вам наскучили нивы бесплодные . . .

10. Чужды вам страсти и чужды страдания . . .
Вечно холодные, вечно свободные,
Нет у вас родины, нет вам изгнания!

Clouds in the sky, eternal wanderers!
Over the azure steppes in a pearly chain
You hasten, like me, seeming exiles,
From the dear North to southern climes.
Who could be driving you: an edict of Fate?
Some hidden envy, or overt malice?
Or does some crime burden you,
Or friends' malicious gossip?
No, you are tired of barren fields . . .
Alien to you are passion and suffering . . .
Eternally cold, eternally free,
You have neither home nor exile!

Thematically the poem is based on a typically Romantic, apparent pathetic fallacy of the poet seeing his own exiled plight in the clouds, yet his own situation is worse because unlike them he is a passionate, suffering human being longing for his homeland. These feelings find tonal expression in the word *тоска*, a combination of sad longing (l.4), bitterness (ll.6 and 8) and despair (l.12).

Structurally this poem falls into three clear parts, each a distinct development: ll.1–4 are an apostrophe to and an apparent identification with the clouds; ll.5–8 a series of rhetorical questions implying the reasons for his own exile; ll.9–12 dispel the apparent identification. Moreover, each section is a quatrain tightly knit by dactylic *abab* rhyme. Its unusual metre – dactylic tetrameter – gives the verse a seductive fluidity, carrying the reader swiftly and easily along. In fact this poem displays a skilful handling of a potentially tedious metre. (Although one should comment on the almost regular pendulum-like movement of the caesura.)

The poem presents us with a blend of natural visual images and abstractions contained within the framework of a metaphor of apparent identification. Its vocabulary is an interesting mixture of the concrete – *тучки; нивы; гонит* – the abstract – *преступление; судьбы ли решение* – the literal – *тучки небесные; нивы бесплодные* – and the figurative. It is dominated by nouns, especially abstractions (ll.5–8), and adjectives. Despite the title and the movement of the verse this is a poem of thought and meditation rather than movement or change (it contains only four verbs). One is, however, impelled to ask – is its phraseology conditioned by the choice of metre? i.e. virtually every noun has an adjective (which fits easily into the ternary scheme, c.f. Longfellow's use of participles in 'Hiawatha') and not always a fortunate one, e.g. what are *тучки* if not *небесные*?; is not *клевета* usually *ядовитая*?

The initial diminutive adds an affective element to the apostrophe of the first line, immediately conveying a tone of sympathy and potential identification. The interplay of *и/н/к/е* makes this a highly mellifluous, eminently recitable introductory line. Yet, is not the adjective *небесные* redundant, and is not *вечные* a virtual cliché? Ozhegov defines *туча* thus: '*Большое, обычно тёмное, густое облако, грозящее какими-то осадками.*' This being so, is the adjective *жемчужною* entirely appropriate, or is it a question of metrical convenience? Nevertheless, there is a strong sense of movement in lines 2–4: a single syntactical unit takes us from *степью* to *южную*; moreover, enjambement contributes to this movement, while the rejet picks out the verb *мчитесь*, thus emphasising this movement. Line 3 is slowed down by commas, giving full metric and rhythmic stress to *будто* and *я*, perhaps questioning the apparently obvious identification. The presence of sibilant consonants in these lines undoubtedly also contributes to their attractive, easy movement.

Lines 5–8 bring a change of pace and focus. Each end-stopped line draws attention to the poet's situation and his romantic self-dramatisation. Regrettably for the poem the supposed causes of exile are the stock-in-trade of Byronic romanticism, i.e. *судьбы ... решение; зависть; злоба; клевета; преступление*. One is almost seduced into acceptance by the movement and mellifluousness of these lines. Line 9 with its stressed *нет* immediately disposes of any sense of identification, although the pathetic fallacy remains in the ascription of feelings, viz. *наскучили*. One is impelled to question the significance and suitability of *бесплодные* except as a device to maintain unity of tone. The abruptness of *нет* is echoed throughout the line in the sound *н*. The suspension points halt the reader and give a brief pause for reflection, and similarly in l.10. Position, metre and rhythm emphasise *чужды*, thus distancing by repetition the clouds even further from the poet's troubles. Considerable similarity in sound gives additional emphasis to the two nouns. The final two lines dispel any possible identification by describing their freedom as lifeless ('cold') and entirely lacking in emotional ties – qualities completely absent in the suffering poet.

On reading this poem one is reminded of Marlowe's 'Come live with me and be my Love' in its fluid, mellifluous movement and 'recitability' being marred by rather clichéd imagery and the pendulum rhythm of the regular caesura.

ЛЕВ НИКОЛА́ЕВИЧ ТОЛСТО́Й

(1828–1910)

Best known for his novels, he also wrote short stories, plays and essays. Apart from his literary work Tolstoy is also important in Russian cultural history as an ethical philosopher and religious reformer. His espousal of non-violent protest had a great influence on M. K. Gandhi. One of four brothers, he was born on the family estate of Yasnaya Polyana, south of Moscow. His mother died in 1830 and the rest of the family moved to Moscow in 1837 for educational reasons. Their father died in the same year and the care of the children passed to their aunts. Nevertheless, Tolstoy had a happy childhood which is reflected in his autobiographical trilogy (q.v. infra).

In 1844 he enrolled at Kazan' University to study Oriental languages but left, bored, in 1847 and returned to Yasnaya Polyana, hoping to improve the condition of his serfs there. In 1851 he went to the Caucasus, joined the army and took part in Russian efforts to suppress the rebellious mountain tribes. During the next year he completed the first volume of his autobiographical trilogy, *Де́тство*. In 1854 he was transferred to Sevastopol and took part in its defence during the Crimean war. During these years he completed several short works, including *Набе́г* (1853), *Отро́чество* (1854), *Ру́бка ле́са* (1855). His greatest success of this period was the so-called 'Sevastopol Stories', viz. *Севасто́поль в декабре́ ме́сяце* (April 1855), *Севасто́поль в ма́е* (June 1855), *Севасто́поль в а́вгусте 1855 го́да* (December 1855). These stories gained him entry into Petersburg literary circles, although his aristocratic aloofness alienated many, including Turgenev (q.v.).

In 1857 he made his first European trip, recording his unfavourable impressions in *Луце́рн*. On his return to Yasnaya Polyana he devoted himself to the education of his peasants' children. In 1862 he married Sofya Behrs, sixteen years younger than himself. He published *Каза́ки* in 1863 and began *Война́ и мир* which took until 1869 to finish. His next major work was *А́нна Каре́нина* during the writing of which, 1873–9, he was tormented by religious doubts; these he described in *И́споведь* (1879). In these two major novels the subtlety with which he depicts and analyses the thoughts and emotions of his characters, and his use of apparently insignificant detail to reveal their inner world are what have justly brought him fame as a great novelist.

Following his rejection of the Russian Orthodox Church and his conversion to a simplified Christianity, Tolstoy concentrated more on religious and philosophical writings than on literature. The fiction he did produce is highly didactic, e.g. *Смерть Ива́на Ильича́* (1886), *Воскресе́ние* (1899). His didacticism is explained in *Что тако́е иску́сство?* (1898).

His ideas, espousal of vegetarianism, chastity, anarchism and non-violence put a great strain on his family life. After years of estrangement from his wife and children (except his youngest daughter Aleksandra) he finally left Yasnaya Polyana in 1910 for an unknown destination, but died unexpectedly at Astapovo station in Ryazan' province.

Анна Каренина
(1873–9)

Степан Аркадьич не избирал ни направления, ни взглядов, а эти направления и взгляды сами приходили к нему, точно так же, как он не выбирал формы шляпы или сюртука, а брал те, которые носят. А иметь взгляды ему, жившему в известном обществе, при потребности некоторой деятельности мысли, развивающейся обыкновенно в лета зрелости, было так же необходимо, как иметь шляпу. Если и была причина, почему он предпочитал либеральное направление консервативному, какого держались тоже многие из его круга, то это произошло не оттого, чтоб он находил либеральное направление более разумным, но потому, что оно подходило ближе к его образу жизни. Либеральная партия говорила, что в России всё дурно, и действительно, у Степана Аркадьича долгов было много, а денег решительно недоставало. Либеральная партия говорила, что брак есть отжившее учреждение и что необходимо перестроить его, и действительно, семейная жизнь доставляла мало удовольствия Степану

Аркадьичу и принуждала его лгать и притворяться, что было так противно его натуре. Либеральная партия говорила, или, лучше, подразумевала, что религия есть только узда для варварской части населения, и действительно, Степан Аркадьич не мог вынести без боли в ногах даже короткого молебна и не мог понять, к чему все эти страшные и высокопарные слова о том свете, когда и на этом жить было бы очень весело. Вместе с этим Степану Аркадьичу, любившему весёлую шутку, было приятно иногда озадачить смирного человека тем, что если уже гордиться породой, то не следует останавливаться на Рюрике и отрекаться от первого родоначальника – обезьяны. Итак, либеральное направление сделалось привычкой Степана Аркадьича, и он любил свою газету, как сигару после обеда, за лёгкий туман, который она производила в его голове.

Stepan Arkad'ich selected neither tendencies nor views, these tendencies and views came to him themselves; in the same way he did not choose the shape of a hat or frock-coat, but wore what everyone else was wearing. Moving in a certain circle where a desire for some form of mental activity was a part of maturity, he was obliged to hold views in the same way as he was obliged to wear a hat. If there was a reason for his preferring the liberal tendency to the conservative one followed by many of his circle, it was not because he thought the liberal one more rational but because it suited his life-style better. The Liberal Party said that everything in Russia was bad and, indeed, Stepan Arkad'ich had many debts and far too little money. The Liberal Party said that marriage was an outmoded institution and should be reformed and, indeed, Stepan Arkad'ich got little pleasure from family life which compelled him to lie and dissemble, which was quite contrary to his nature. The Liberal Party said or, rather, implied that religion was only a way of curbing the barbaric section of the populace and, indeed, Stepan Arkad'ich could not stand even the shortest church-service without getting aching feet and could not understand all those frightful and high-flown words about the other world, when it was really quite nice living in this one. Sometimes it also amused Stepan Arkad'ich, who enjoyed a good joke, to shock a conventional person by saying that, if one prides oneself on one's birth, one ought not to stop at Rurik nor renounce one's earliest ancestors – the apes. Thus, the liberal tendency became a habit for Stepan Arkad'ich and he enjoyed his newspaper, as he did his after-dinner cigar, for the slight haze it produced in his head.

In this descriptive passage we are given Stiva Oblonsky's 'views' on life and society, a passage pervaded by a carefully controlled irony. This irony is conveyed syntactically by direct comparison, e.g. *Он любил свою газету, как сигару после обеда, за лёгкий туман, который она производила в его голове*; by implication through repetition, e.g. *Либеральная партия говорила, что в России всё дурно, и действительно, у Степана Аркадьича долгов было много* ...; and by diction, e.g. *взгляды* сами *приходили к нему; жившему в* известном *обществе в лета зрелости; Если и была причина; Либеральная партия* говорила; и действительно; *а денег* решительно *недоставало*.

Irony is reinforced by the skilful development of content. The general statement, containing the direct equivalence of convictions and clothes, is amplified until a final summarising sentence. Specifically, the first two sentences concern the equivalence of clothing and convictions. There follows a general reason for his 'choice' of liberal views, which is amplified by four examples. A final sentence summarises the meaning of liberalism to Stiva. Overall unity is maintained by subject-matter and tone.

The vocabulary of the passage is elaborate and sophisticated, using abstract and concrete freely, yet avoiding imagery and figurative usage. Thus, the passage appeals entirely to the intellect and imagination in its conveying of Stiva's attitudes; his physical presence is virtually absent. There is a more or less equal balance of nouns and verbs and, although there are relatively few adverbs and adjectives, they do contribute decisively to tone and meaning, e.g. *известном; дурно; противно; весёлую/очень весело; действительно*. These are combined into very simple but effective, ironic phrases, e.g. *все эти страшные и высокопарные слова; даже короткого молебна; было бы очень весело; при потребности некоторой деятельности мысли*.

The multiple antithesis and syntax of the first two introductory sentences establish the unifying theme, tone and rhythm of the whole passage. The double antithesis of the first long sentence effectively equates Stepan Arkad'ich's passivity in both clothing and convictions. The elements of the first clause are virtually reversed in the second, thus making Stepan Arkad′ich their object, thereby giving syntactic expression to his passivity: *Степан Аркадьич не избирал ни направления, ни взглядов, а эти направления и взгляды сами приходили к нему.*

The use of *точно так же* extends this passivity into the very clothing he wears. Although at the end of the sentence syntactic expression is different, the effect is the same, i.e. the active *брал те* is cancelled out by the passive *которые носят*, the overall effect being the equation of views and tendencies with hats and coats. Antithesis also extends to the use of the negative, i.e. the repeated balancing of negative/positive. Similarly, by syntactic balance the two verbs *избирал/ выбирал* are equated. The linking particle *a* acts as a thematic link to the following sentence, typically Tolstoyan in its complex syntax. Here, multiple subordination and cumulative rhythm are used with devastating effect: the phrase *А иметь взгляды ему* is qualified by three ponderous phrases, probably Stepan Arkad′ich's own words, and the pregnant *было так же необходимо* crashing into the bathetic irony of *как иметь шляпу.* The vocabulary of these phrases is carefully chosen: empty, pompous periphrasis: *в известном обществе; при потребности некоторой деятельности мысли; развивающейся обыкновенно в лета зрелости.*

In dealing with Stepan Arkad′ich's 'choice' of liberal views, expectations are built up by a similar rhythmic and equally complex syntax: *Если и была причина,* почему *он предпочитал либеральное направление консервативному,* какого *держались тоже многие из его круга,* то это произошло не оттого, чтоб *он находил либеральное направление более разумным* ... builds up to the clause *но потому, что оно подходило ближе к его образу жизни* – a great wave breaking into a puddle. The pregnant *и* after *если* subtly questions the whole discussion of Stepan Arkad′ich's 'views'. The apparently redundant repetition of *либеральное направление* probably echoes Stepan Arkad′ich's equally redundant use of it.

Tolstoy then amplifies these liberal views and how they suit Stepan Arkad′ich's life-style. Yet how does he make this extensive section so sharply ironic? – by the repeated parallelism and rhythmic effect of a ponderous political statement, e.g. *брак есть отжившее учреждение; религия есть только узда для варварской части населения* being balanced by two mundane statements about his likes and dislikes. The effect of this is heightened still further by the careful placing and/or repetition of adverbs or phrases like *и действительно; решительно; мало; так противно; или, лучше, подразумевала; даже короткого молебна; все эти страшные и высокопарные слова; было бы очень весело.* Apart from its convenience the 'liberal tendency' allows him to make a 'good joke'. At this point irony is conveyed by choice of words, viz. *вместе с этим; любившему весёлую шутку; было приятно иногда.*

Finally, in the last sentence, Tolstoy does not simply summarise the nature of Stepan Arkad'ich's 'convictions' but, in uncharacteristically simple language and syntax, draws a direct comparison between the effect of 'his newspaper' and a cigar on Stepan Arkad'ich – both are mildly and pleasantly narcotic.

АФАНА́СИЙ АФАНА́СИЕВИЧ ФЕТ

(1820–92)

Born in the Orlov district of central Russia in 1820, he used his German mother's name, Foeth, until 1873, when he adopted his father's name Shenshin. He was educated at a German boarding-school in Estonia and at Moscow University from 1838 to 1844, after which he entered the army. His first collection of poems, *Лири́ческий пантео́н*, was published in 1840 and another, *Стихотворе́ния*, in 1850.

After travels abroad he married a wealthy woman in 1856 and befriended Turgenev and Tolstoy. He retired to a farm in 1862 and wrote conservative articles which infuriated the Radicals. In 1881 he moved to Moscow where he occupied himself with translations from Latin and German, his own poetry collected in *Вече́рние огни́* (1883) and his prose memoirs. He attempted suicide and died of heart failure.

Fet's striking nature- and love-lyrics reflect his total concern with Beauty and Art in an age dominated by novelists and radical critics demanding social awareness in literature.

> Как здесь свежо под липою густою, –
> Полдневный зной сюда не проникал,
> И тысячи висящих надо мною
> Качаются душистых опахал.
>
> А там вдали сверкает воздух жгучий,
> Колебляся, как будто дремлет он.
> Так резко-сух снотворный и трескучий
> Кузнечиков неугомонный звон.
>
> За мглой ветвей синеют неба своды,
> Как дымкою подёрнуты слегка,
> И, как мечты почиющей природы,
> Волнистые проходят облака.
>
> (1854)

How cool it is here beneath a leafy lime, –
The heat of midday does not reach here,
And hanging above me wave
Thousands of fragrant fans.

Out there in the distance glitters the burning air,
Swaying as though drowsing.
The soporific whirring and indefatigable chirring
Of grasshoppers is so shrilly desiccated.

Beyond the branches' gloom is the blue vault of heaven,
Seeming slightly smoky,
And, like slumbering Nature's dreams,
Wavy clouds sail by.

Because of similarities with the contemporary French 'Parnasse' Fet has been called the 'Russian Parnassian'. The similarities are very much evident in this poem which, rather than being 'about' anything, is a sensuous appreciation of a moment through art.

Because of the poem's deliberate impersonality the author's 'voice' is muted. However, feeling is conveyed through an intense sensuous awareness and delight, e.g. *как здесь свежо; тысячи висящих надо мною/качаются душистых опахал; сверкает воздух жгучий; так резко-сух; неугомонный звон; дымкою подёрнуты слегка.* Lacking a theme, the poem also lacks any obvious structural development, except in so far as the first two lines set the scene. Fet presents a series of images rendered more vivid by a stanza form, i.e. the cool, scented air beneath a lime-tree; the shimmering air ringing with chirring grasshoppers; a cloud-flecked sky. Moreover, the vividness of this moment is heightened by the poem's consisting of only three quatrains, while its seductively rhyming iambic pentameters entirely avoid metre/rhythm counterpoint.

The poem *is* in fact its imagery, not a clothing of thought in images. Despite its date of writing this poem approaches music and non-representational art in being a self-subsistent statement. Its vocabulary is markedly simple and concrete, with only one abstraction – *мечты* – in the one simile, while metaphor is unobtrusively 'dead': *опахал; звон; почиющей.* For this reason sensuous appeal marks the poem, appealing to the visual, aural and olfactory. Appropriately, it is a very static poem dominated by nouns and adjectives; with the exception of *качаются* even the verbs contribute to this vision: *проходят*, in this context, is virtually static. However, the poem is rescued from potential indifference by the galvanising effect of its phraseology which considerably heightens the images: *душистых опахал; воздух жгучий; резко-сух снотворный и трескучий.*

The first line presents the vantage-point of the author's observations – its end-stopped line effectively introduces the situation, but also creates tension through a desire for amplification, especially because of the dash. The movement of this line is remarkably fluid because metric- and word-stress coincide and only 'little' words are used. The second line explains the vantage-point – a cool refuge from the intense noonday heat. These two lines present a carefully balanced contrast because the implied caesuras after *свежо* and *зной* contrast the two images. The impact of ll.3 and 4, a single syntactic unit, is greater because ll.1 and 2 are end-stopped. This impact operates on several levels: the combination of verse movement and sound from *и* to *опахал*; metric-stress pattern is different from ll.1 and 2 because the three effective stresses in each line on the polysyllabic words create a large number of short, unstressed vowels (*и/о/а/э*), thus altering the verse movement while emphasising in the stressed long vowels the acoustic element of *качаются* (the consonants *с/ч/ш/щ* also contribute to this); syntactically, the initial placing of *тысячи* and final placing of *опахал* (providing a useful clinching rhyme) do add to the line's impressive movement.

The second stanza is devoted to the visual and aural quality of the air. Lines 5 and 6 seek to convey its shimmering vibrancy. An unusual number of verbs emphasises this, viz. *сверкает; колебляся; дремлет.* The relatively neutral *а там вдали* transfers the emphasis to *сверкает* and an implied caesura picks out *воздух жгучий*, the end-stopping comma drawing attention to this unusual adjective. The consonant clusters throughout the line serve to make the impact of *воздух жгучий* very strong. A skilfully placed comma isolates *колебляся*, making the reader pause to consider the whole image summoned up by it, as does its labio-liquid articulation. The *л* and *е* in this gerund are picked up by the other significant word *дремлет*, itself a verb. This is the first of a number of personifications whereby the noonday natural world is almost akin to someone drowsing and dreaming in the heat. The abrupt sound and movement of these two lines is in marked contrast with the quiescence of the verbless, highly imagistic ll.7 and 8. The complex effect of the incessant chirring of the grasshoppers is conveyed by the striking adjectival line: *так резко-сух снотворный и трескучий*, each word bearing metric and rhythmic stress. Sound pattern is used here to good effect: the consonants *к/х/m/р* being appropriate to the chirring of grasshoppers while the long *у* and *o* convey the soporific effect of the unceasing noise. The same effect continues into l.8 (*к/г/з/н*) where, by syntactic inversion and metric stress, the echoing *неугомонный звон* is highlighted.

Different again is the final stanza, syntactically echoing the first with the use of the conjunction in l.11 but, nevertheless, subtly different in emphasis and movement: the very prominent vowel sounds of l.11: *ой/ей/ею/e/o* overshadowing the alliterated *c* and *в*, seem eminently suited to the image of a blue sky, contrasting with the shade. This liquid movement changes to a more dactylic rhythm, with its harsher *к/х/д*, to draw attention to a barely perceptible haze. This changes again to the long words and flowing anapaestic rhythm of ll.11 and 12 where the passing clouds are the noonday dreams of a personified slumbering Nature, given acoustic equivalence in the vowels *u/o* and the consonants *n/p*.

ФЁДОР МИХА́ЙЛОВИЧ ДОСТОЕ́ВСКИЙ

(1821–81)

Dostoevsky was born in Moscow, the son of a doctor and the second of eight children. He enrolled in the Military Engineering School in Petersburg in 1837, in the same year as his mother died. By this time he was already short of money – a lifelong problem. He resigned the army in 1844 to become a writer. His epistolary novel, *Бе́дные лю́ди*, published in 1846, was highly acclaimed by the radical critics, especially Belinsky. His next work, *Двойни́к*, appearing a few weeks later, did not meet with such approval. This disappointment was aggravated by the onset of chronic epilepsy. Involvement with the Petrashevsky circle led to his arrest and exile for four years in 1849 to a labour camp near Omsk, followed by a further four years in the army. These traumatic years brought him into contact with the Russian lower classes and Christianity. The fruits of his experiences are recorded with great restraint in *Запи́ски из мёртвого до́ма* (1860–2).

He returned to Petersburg in 1859 and in 1861 his clumsy and far less impressive novel, *Уни́женные и оскорблённые*, began to be serialised in his brother Mikhail's journal, *Вре́мя*. He worked with his brother on this journal from 1861 to 1863 and then on its successor, *Эпо́ха*, from 1864 to 1865. In 1862 he visited Europe and the London Crystal Palace, recording his highly unfavourable impressions in *Зи́мние заме́тки о ле́тних впечатле́ниях*. This was followed by his short novel, *Запи́ски из подпо́лья*, in 1864, considered by many as a twentieth-century work in its probing of the dark recesses of the mind.

Heavily in debt and prostrated by the death of his beloved brother Mikhail, Dostoevsky nevertheless managed to produce his first great novel, *Преступле́ние и наказа́ние*, in 1866. Permanently on the run from creditors he lived in Western Europe, yet was able to produce *Идио́т* in 1869 and *Бе́сы* in

1872. On his return to Russia in 1871 he became a famous religious conservative figure and, for the first time, solvent. In 1879–80 his greatest and longest work, *Бра́тья Карама́зовы*, was published.

Although Dostoevsky's novels lack the structural perfection of Turgenev's, the issues dealt with in them are ahead of their author's time in being ultimately a form of religious existentialism: in order for Man to know himself truly, he must question everything, know evil and experience great suffering.

Преступление и наказание

(1866)

На улице жара стояла страшная, к тому же духота, толкотня, всюду известка, леса, кирпич, пыль и та особенная летняя вонь, столь известная каждому петербуржцу, не имеющему возможности нанять дачу, – всё это разом неприятно потрясло и без того уже расстроенные нервы юноши. Нестерпимая же вонь из распивочных, которых в этой части города особенное множество, и пьяные, поминутно попадавшиеся, несмотря на буднее время, довершили отвратительный и грустный колорит картины. Чувство глубочайшего омерзения мелькнуло на миг в тонких чертах молодого человека. Кстати, он был замечательно хорош собою, с прекрасными тёмными глазами, темнорус, ростом выше среднего, тонок и строен. Но скоро он впал как бы в глубокую задумчивость, даже, вернее сказать, как бы в какое-то забытьё, и пошёл, уже не замечая окружающего, да и не желая его замечать. Изредка бормотал он что-то про себя, от своей привычки к монологам, в которой он сам себе признался. В эту же минуту он и сам сознавал, что мысли его порою мешаются и что он очень слаб: второй день как уж он почти совсем ничего не ел.

Он был до того худо одет, что иной, даже и привычный человек, посовестился бы днём выходить в таких лохмотьях на улицу. Впрочем, квартал был таков, что костюмом здесь было трудно кого-нибудь удивить. Близость Сенной, обилие известных заведений и, по преимуществу, цеховое и ремесленное население, скученное в этих серединных петербургских улицах и переулках, пестрили иногда общую панораму такими субъектами, что странно было бы и удивляться при встрече с иною фигурой. Но столько злобного презрения уже накопилось в душе молодого человека, что, несмотря на всю свою, иногда очень молодую, щекотливость, он менее всего совестился своих лохмотьев на улице.

The heat on the street was frightful, moreover the closeness, the crowds, the mortar, scaffolding and bricks everywhere, the dust and that peculiar summer stench so well known to everyone living in Petersburg who cannot afford to rent a country cottage – all these things at once had a very unpleasant effect on the young man's already overwrought nerves. The unbearable stench from the pubs, of which there are a particularly large number in that part of town, and the frequent drunks, despite its being a weekday, gave the finishing touch to this sad and revolting picture. For a moment an expression of deep loathing passed across the young man's fine features. He was, incidentally, remarkably handsome with beautiful dark eyes, dark brown hair, above average height, slim and well-built. But soon he sank into a deep reverie or, more precisely, into a kind of oblivion, and walked on no longer aware of his surroundings, nor for that matter wishing to be. Occasionally he would mumble something to himself because of his habit of talking to himself – a habit of which he was himself aware. At that moment he was also aware that his thoughts were getting confused and that he felt very weak: for two days now he had scarcely had anything to eat.

He was so badly dressed that anybody else, even if accustomed to it, would have been ashamed to go out in such rags during the day. However, it would have been difficult in that part of town to surprise anyone by what one was wearing. The proximity of the Hay Market, the large number of brothels and especially the working-class population crammed into these central Petersburg streets and alleys provided such an abundance of odd characters that it would have been strange to be surprised at meeting anyone. Yet so much bitter contempt had already accumulated in the young man's heart that, despite his occasionally very youthful punctiliousness about dress, he was least of all ashamed of his rags in the street.

This introductory descriptive passage sets the scene, both physically and psychologically, for the novel. By definition the early, introductory scenes of a novel need to command the reader's attention and create the desire to read on. How does Dostoevsky achieve this? A tone of tension and mystery is created by syntactic and linguistic means. The long initial sentence accumulates detail upon unpleasant detail and, at the sentence's climax, diction intimates both a sense of mystery and disturbance, i.e. the protagonist is simply referred to as *юноша* and his mental state suggested by the phrase *потрясло и без того расстроенные нервы.*

Further on he is simply referred to as *молодой человек* and such words and phrases as *задумчивость; забытьё; уже не замечая окружающего; своей привычки к монологам* increase still further the mystery of his mental state. Repeated qualification intensifies the mood: *даже; вернее сказать; да и не желая; впрочем; несмотря на.*

Structural organisation increases the impact of this introduction. The passage as a whole operates by contrast and accumulation, the basic pattern of which is evident in the first sentence – the author switches from the outer world of the slums of St Petersburg to the disturbed inner world of the unknown young man. The two paragraphs amplify this, accumulating detail about the sordid district and describing the young man's intense mental disturbance. This contrast also operates on a secondary level of implication – that between his implied social origins and his sordid environment and ragged clothing. This structure is held together by unity of tone and subject-matter, viz. the whole piece is pervaded by the mystery and suspense of this demented, well-bred young man wandering in the slums.

The passage's dominant imagery is that of overwhelming unpleasantness: *жара страшная; духота; вонь; пьяные, поминутно попадавшиеся; обилие известных заведений.* Since this passage deals with the outer and the inner worlds, the vocabulary range comprises the concrete and the abstract, the sensuous and the intellectual. The first sentence illustrates this well. An overwhelming predominance of nouns and adjectives gives a striking, if somewhat static, Breughelesque reality to this description. Verbs, when used, have a somewhat abstract quality and mainly relate to the young man's state of mind: *потрясло и без того уже расстроенные нервы; чувство глубочайшего омерзения мелькнуло; он впал как бы в задумчивость; он и сам сознавал; он менее всего совестился.*

Phraseology plays an extremely important part in creating the tone and the sense of reality of both the inner and the outer worlds, e.g. the overall sordidity of the area: *нестерпимая вонь; отвратительный и грустный колорит; пьяные, поминутно попадавшиеся;* the young man's mental state: *расстроенные нервы; чувство глубочайшего омерзения; столько злобного презрения;* the mystery of his being in the slums: *замечательно хорош собою; ростом выше среднего; всю свою, иногда очень молодую, щекотливость.*

The very first sentence of the passage makes a decisive impact in setting the physical and mental scenes. Apart from the static verb *стояла* one is assailed by nouns and adjectives piling up the details of the customary summer sordidity of the district. Its cumulative rhythm is suddenly stopped by the comma and dash to emphasise what follows. The words are carefully chosen: the total impact: *всё это разом;* its nature: *неприятно потрясло;* the mental instability of the subject: *и без того уже расстроенные нервы юноши.* The sordidity is increased still more in the following sentence by diction: the smell is *нестерпимая;* the number of pubs – *особенное множество;* the number of drunks – *поминутно попадавшиеся,* and by syntax, i.e. qualification by a subordinate clause: *которых в этой части города особенное множество,* or dependent phrase: *пьяные, поминутно попадавшиеся, несмотря на буднее время,* and parallel subjects of the verb *довершили,* i.e. *вонь* and *пьяные,* both with a balancing dependent clause and phrase.

The effect, mentioned above, on the youth is also intensified by a further sentence, *Чувство глубочайшего омерзения мелькнуло на миг в тонких чертах молодого человека,* which parallels and balances *всё это разом неприятно потрясло и без того уже расстроенные нервы юноши.* Yet it also heightens the suspense – his fine features and delicate feelings are so obviously out of place in this district: this is emphasised by the use of the superlative *глубочайший.* It also changes the focus from the environment to the young man and his state of mind. The mystery is deepened by a brief interpolation on his striking physical appearance: he is *замечательно хорош собою,* his eyes are *прекрасными,* his stature *выше среднего.* His strange mental state is emphasised again by the device of syntactic qualification, i.e. he is not simply pensive but *вернее сказать, как бы в какое-то забытьё;* he is not simply unaware of his surroundings but *не желая его замечать.*

A fluid sense of time is intimated by certain phrases: *но скоро; изредка; в эту же минуту*. The mystery of his condition deepens until the very end of the paragraph. What is his *привычка к монологам*? Why is he *очень слаб*? The impact of the final sentence is all the greater since, unlike those preceding, it is a single rhythmic and syntactic unit. Moreover, word-order adds further emphasis by the placing at the end of the verb and its object *ничего не ел*.

The second paragraph continues to dwell on the stranger, this time on his shabby appearance, again emphasised by the device of qualification: *даже и привычный человек*. Just as Dostoevsky had changed the focus in the first paragraph with *кстати*, with *впрочем* he returns to the stranger's surroundings. As in the first sentence, their oppressive presence is given syntactic equivalence, i.e. the cumulative rhythm of the compound subject of the verb *пестрили*. The whole situation is heightened in this paragraph by a number of conjunctions: *до того ... что; таков, что; такими, что; столько, что*, as it is in the final mysterious sentence by *столько; уже; несмотря на всю свою; менее всего* – all of which emphasise the degree of these feelings and appearances.

НИКОЛА́Й АЛЕКСЕ́ЕВИЧ НЕКРА́СОВ

(1821–77)

Nekrasov was born in 1821 and spent his boyhood on his father's estate in Yaroslavl' province on the Upper Volga. His father was a coarse, debauched tyrant, and his mother a gentle, well-educated Polish woman. She died when he was still quite young and he greatly cherished her memory. He was sent to Petersburg in 1838 to train as an army officer but, disobeying his father, attended classes at the University and published a poem, *Мысль*, in a journal. Disowned by his angry father, he could not afford to continue and was compelled to take odd jobs and live in dire poverty for three years. His poems, *Мечты и звуки* (1840), were a failure and he destroyed them. His fortunes then improved, and by 1845 he was established as a publisher, editing *Петербургский сборник* with Herzen, and had become a friend of Belinsky. In 1846 he purchased and revived *Современник*, which had been founded by Pushkin, and transformed it into the chief Russian radical review of the mid nineteenth century. In it he published, besides his own poems, stories by Turgenev, L. N. Tolstoy and others.

During the 1850s Nekrasov drew closer to the more radical critics and writers, especially Chernyshevsky and Dobrolyubov, driving away Turgenev and other liberals. In March 1862 he became the sole owner of *Современник* in which, in January 1864, appeared *Моро́з, Кра́сный нос*. By then he had become Russia's most popular poet, especially among the radical and liberal intelligentsia, but after the attempted assassination of Alexander II in 1866 his journal was closed down, despite his cringing attitude to the authorities.

In 1868, now disliked by both radicals and conservatives, he took over *Отечественные записки*, collaborating with Saltykov-Shchedrin. By a policy of greater caution he managed to keep this going until his greatly mourned death from cancer in 1877. In his last years he produced his most ambitious long poem, *Кому́ на Руси́ жить хорошо́?* (1876). He is *the* nineteenth-century Russian poet of the *наро́д*, depicting with true emotion and intimate knowledge the frightful sufferings of 'his incredibly patient nation', yet seeing hope in the Russian land and its people's simple faith.

Мороз, Красный нос
(1864)

1/1
'Вглядись, молодица, смелее,
Каков воевода Мороз!
Навряд тебе парня сильнее
И краше видать привелось?

2/5
Метели, снега и туманы
Покорны морозу всегда,
Пойду на моря-окияны –
Построю дворцы изо льда.

3/9
Задумаю – реки большие
Надолго упрячу под гнёт,
Построю мосты ледяные,
Каких не построит народ.

4/13
Где быстрые, шумные воды
Недавно свободно текли, –
Сегодня прошли пешеходы,
Обозы с товаром прошли.

5/17
Люблю я в глубоких могилах
Покойников в иней рядить,
И кровь вымораживать в жилах,
И мозг в голове леденить.

6/21
На го́ре недоброму вору,
На страх седоку и коню,
Люблю я в вечернюю пору
Затеять в лесу трескотню.

7/25
Бабёнки, пеняя на леших,
Домой удирают скорей.
А пьяных, и конных, и пеших
Дурачить ещё веселей.

8/29

Без мелу всю выбелю рожу,
А нос запылает огнём,
И бороду так приморожу
К вожжам – хоть руби топором!

9/33

Богат я, казны не считаю,
А всё не скудеет добро;
Я царство моё убираю
В алмазы, жемчуг, серебро.

10/37

Войди в моё царство со мною
И будь ты царицею в нём!
Поцарствуем славно зимою,
А летом глубоко уснём.

11/41

Войди! приголублю, согрею,
Дворец отведу голубой . . .'
И стал воевода над нею
Махать ледяной булавой.

'Come and look, young wife, more boldly,
Come and see Lord Frost!
Have you ever chanced to see
A lad more handsome and more powerful?

Storms, snows and mists
Always bow to Frost,
I may go to seas and oceans –
There I'll build palaces all of ice.

If I've a mind, the mighty rivers
I'll hide away for ages underneath my weight,
I'll build bridges all of ice,
Which no man could ever build.

Where the swift and noisy waters
Recently flowed freely, –
People walked across today,
And laden wagon-trains passed over.

Down in deep graves I like decking
Dead men out in hoar-frost white,
Chilling and freezing blood in the veins,
And in your head freezing up the brains.

To bring to grief the wicked thief,
And frighten horse and rider,
I do like at evening tide
Making strange sounds in the forest.

Young women, blaming wood sprites,
Rush off home in haste.
While drinkers and riders and walkers
Are even better to fool with.

I can whiten a mug without chalk,
And set your nose a-burning,
And freeze a beard so hard to the reins
You'd have to hack it off!

I'm a wealthy man, I don't count my cash,
Nor do my goods run short;
I deck out my kingdom
All in silver, diamonds, pearls.

Enter in my kingdom with me
And in it be my queen!
We'll rule well through winter,
And sleep all summer long.

Come enter! I'll caress and warm you,
Allot you my pale-blue palace . . .'
So saying Lord Frost began
To brandish his icy mace above her.

In this excerpt personified Frost describes his immense, non-human powers in order to impress and seduce the freezing woman. The exultation, panache and humour ascribed to Lord Frost are conveyed in such expressions and lines as: *парня сильнее и краше; пойду на моря-окияны – /построю дворцы изо льда* and the whole of stanzas 6, 7 and 9. As a whole it could be said to have a cumulative structure of seduction: the first stanza is a self-apostrophe; stanzas 2–4 state his great powers; 5–8 show the humorous aspects of these powers, and 9–11 are an invitation to reign in this great kingdom.

The stanzaic structure makes clearer each of his claims. Each one of the eleven falls into two parts – altogether surely making him irresistible! In a highly appropriate but not naive imitation of folk poetry (viz. four lines of one iambic and two anapaestic feet rhyming *abab*) the metric regularity contributes to his efforts by lulling the listener into acceptance. Its imagery is that of nineteenth-century rural Russia in winter: snow, frost, ice, peasants, horses, carts and wood-sprites – all conveyed by a simple, concrete, literal and largely visual vocabulary devoid of metaphor and simile. A predominance of nouns gives a great sense of reality to this picture of rural Russia, while its wide variety of verbs imparts vigour to the scene. Its phraseology is highly conventional, as befits a pseudo-folk narrative, e.g. *парня сильнее и краше; реки большие; в глубоких могилах, недоброму вору; поцарствуем славно; хоть руби топором.*

The rural 'feel' of the excerpt is evident from the first stanza with such words as *молодица; воевода; парня; краше.* The typical movement of the verse, very different from other poems considered, is well exemplified in the first stanza. The minimal use of metre/rhythm counterpoint imparts, by giving full stress value to all the significant words, a great fluidity to the verse movement, but with a danger of 'Hiawatha' tedium. Similarly typical of this extract is the sequence of two end-stopped lines and two others forming a single syntactical unit. The resultant song-like effect of these devices provides an interesting contrast to Tyutchev's 'Silentium' (q.v.). Nekrasov is eminently declaimable, a quality beloved of Russians.

In the first stanza the isolation of l.2 highlights Frost' self-apostrophe, while the uninterrupted movement of ll.3 and 4 allows the linkage of *сильнее/и краше*, the feminine rhyme picking out *сильнее/смелее.* Throughout this stanza there is a complex system of sibilant, liquid and guttural consonance *с/з/ц/ш; г/к/л*, and a notable system of vowel relationships: *и/е* in l.1, *о* in l.2 and *а/я* in ll.3 and 4. Stanza 2 achieves a fine balance of elements: his power over natural forces, represented by the three nouns in l.5 (appropriately rhymed with another aspect of Nature in the folk-tautology *моря/окияны*), is emphasised by the verse movement and the placing of *покорны* and *всегда*, echoed to great effect by the strong masculine rhyme - *льда.* Lines 7 and 8, both end-stopped and thereby compelling the reader's attention, emphasise still further his power by beginning each line with a first person verb: *пойду* and *построю*, both of which echo the *по-* of l.6.

Line 9 in stanza 3 draws attention to Frost in a simila

manner, but this 'habitual' perfective future acquires maximum emphasis by an almost casual interpolation of a dash, creating an unusual counterpoint of metre and rhythm, and the subsequent uninterrupted movement to *гнёт*. Perhaps the consonant clusters of l.10 may be seen as a phonetic expression of the constricting effect of the ice. The two end-stopped lines 11 and 12 form a strong antithesis: *построю* at the beginning of l.11 reasserts Frost's power over water, while the limp *народ* at the end of l.12 contrasts Man's relative powerlessness. A similar antithesis extends to the whole of stanza 4. In ll.13 and 14 the powerful flow of water (conveyed by uninterrupted and metrically exact verse movement, normal syntax and a diapason of vowel sounds – *ы/у/а/о/и*) is suddenly halted by a comma and dash. Antithesis extends to the repeated *прошли*, exploiting the sounds *п/р/в/ш/о/а*.

Moving on from his power over water, Lord Frost changes to a humorous tone, describing his ideas of 'fun', viz. freezing solid the living and the dead. The three end-stopped lines 18–20, with their syntactic objects given the first metric stress, impart a certain abruptness to each statement, as do the recurrent gutturals *г/к/х*. The 'larks' continue into stanza 6, where ll.21 and 22 achieve their effect by the initial placing of the phrases *на горе* and *на страх*, and by the end-stopping of the lines. In final position, clinched by rhyme and highly onomatopoeic, *трескотню* creates a strong and, unique in this extract, auditory image. The same 'scare tactics' are extended into stanza 7 with Frost's contemptuous choice of words – *бабёнки; удирают; дурачить*. Lines 25 and 27 have an unusual movement in that a certain jerky counterpoint is set up by the commas, but it does highlight the nouns. Another interesting feature is the contrast in movement of these lines with ll.26 and 28 which are both more fluid in movement and sound, and connect through rhyme. Maintaining the same humorous and slightly contemptuous tone (N.B. *рожу*) in stanza 8, in ll.29 and 30 *рожу* and *нос* are emphasised by position, the vowels *у/ю* and *a/o* imparting a characteristic sound to each. Similarly *бороду* has positional emphasis, while the 'folksy' *хоть руби топором* is highlighted by the preceding momentary pause. The humour is to some extent emphasised by the slight absurdity of the phrases *запылает огнём* and *хоть руби топором*.

Having presumably overwhelmed his victim with the relating of his powers through eight stanzas, Lord Frost completes the seduction with a lavish description of his wealth to be shared, beginning immediately with *богат* in 1.33, pinpointed by the comma pause which also emphasises the rather archaic *казны*, imparting a medieval flavour. In the same way *царство* receives positional emphasis, while rhythm emphasises the three nouns in 1.36, aided by rhyme which links *добро* with *серебро*. The 'invitation' in stanza 10 is delivered with great panache as the verse sweeps from the emphatic *войди* past the alluring *царицею* to *в нём!*, aided by the sounds *ц/т/с/в* and the vowel range of *у/о/а/у*. With great metric agility Nekrasov places the strikingly emphatic *поцарствуем* at the beginning of 1.39. Lines 39 and 40 are exact antitheses and achieve their emphases thereby: *уснём* stands at the end, *поцарствуем* at the beginning, *летом* at the end, *зимою* at the beginning. This appropriately emphasises that they, unlike ordinary mortals, will be most active in winter, not summer. The final stanza repeats the verb *войди* with extra emphasis from the exclamation mark and full-stop. A further two (highly ironic in this context) verbs accumulate his promises, each highlighted by rhythmic counterpoint and punctuation.

ИВА́Н АЛЕКСЕ́ЕВИЧ БУ́НИН

(1870–1953)

Born into an ancient, but impoverished, noble family in Voronezh, Bunin studied at Moscow University and then worked for the rural administration in central Russia. He was acquainted with Chekhov and joined Gor′ky's group of writers in the late 1890s, and for more than ten years all his works were published by the *Зна́ние* publishing house, but he never identified himself with its political elements. In the years preceding the First World War, Bunin travelled much in Mediterranean and tropical countries. Many of his works are dated from Capri. In 1917 he took a very strong anti-Bolshevik stand and emigrated in 1918. From 1919 until his death he lived in France, a leading member of the First Emigration. Despite his political views Bunin has received cautious acceptance in the Soviet Union since the 1960s.

His first volume of poetry was published in 1891, a collection of descriptive nature lyrics in the tradition of Fet (q.v.) and entirely ignoring the contemporary Symbolist movement. In 1901 he received the Pushkin Prize for his nature poem, *Листопа́д*. In the early years of his literary career he did a great deal of translation from English, especially a complete Russian version of 'The Song of Hiawatha'.

He is primarily famous for his prose in which he was concerned with the decay of Russian rural life at the end of the nineteenth century, conveyed through an exquisitely objective, cold and aloof prose. Typical works are *Дере́вня* (1910), *Суходо́л* (1911), *Грамма́тика любви́* (1915), *Сны Ча́нга* (1924). However, he is probably most well-known for his thematically untypical *Господи́н из Сан-франци́ско* (1922), a powerful and pessimistic satire on Western bourgeois civilisation, while probably his best and only partially translated work is his fictionalised autobiography, *Жизнь Арсе́ньева* (1928–33), for which he received a highly disputed Nobel Prize in 1933. He is unusual in twentieth-century Russian literature in continuing the nineteenth-century critical-realist tradition in a precise rhythmic and uniquely evocative prose, although his influence is noticeable among the new generation of writers, especially Kazakov (q.v.).

Далёкое

(1924)

Москва прожила свою сложную и утомительную зиму. А потом прожила Великий пост, Пасху и опять почувствовала, будто она что-то кончила, что-то свалила с плеч, дождалась чего-то настоящего. И было множество москвичей, которые уже меняли или готовились изменить свою жизнь, начать её как бы сначала и уже по-иному, чем прежде, зажить разумнее, правильнее, моложе и спешили убирать квартиры, заказывать летние костюмы, делать покупки – а ведь покупать (даже нафталин) весело! – готовились, одним словом, к отъезду из Москвы, к отдыху на дачах, на Кавказе, в Крыму, за границей, вообще к лету, которое, как всегда кажется, непременно должно быть счастливым и долгим, долгим.

Сколько прекрасных, радующих душу чемоданов и новеньких, скрипящих корзин было куплено тогда в Леонтьевском переулке и у Мюра-Мерилиза! Сколько народу стриглось, брилось у Базиля и Теодора! И один за другим шли солнечные, возбуждающие дни, дни с новыми запахами, с новой чистотой улиц, с новым блеском церковных маковок на ярком небе, с новым Страстным, с новой Петровкой, с новыми светлыми нарядами на щеголихах и красавицах, пролетавших на лёгких лихачах по Кузнецкому, с новой светлосерой шляпой знаменитого актёра, тоже быстро пролетавшего куда-то на 'дутых'. Все кончали какую-то полосу своей прежней, не той, какой нужно было, жизни, и чуть не для всей Москвы был канун жизни новой, непременно счастливой – был он и у меня даже особенно, гораздо больше других, как казалось мне тогда. И всё близился и близился срок моей разлуки с 'Северным полюсом', со всем тем, чем жил я в нём по-студенчески, и с утра до вечера был я в хлопотах, в разъездах по Москве, во всяческих радостных заботах. А что же делл мой сосед по номерам, скромнейший современник наш? Да

приблизительно то же, что и мы. С ним случилось в конце концов
то же самое, что и со всеми нами.

Moscow had gone through its complicated and tiring winter.
Then, having got through Lent and Easter, began to feel again
that it had finished something, got rid of something and that
something real had happened. There were very many Muscovites who had already changed or were preparing to change
their lives, to begin as it were from the beginning and in a
different way from before, to start living more reasonably,
more correctly and in a younger fashion, and made haste to
tidy their flats, to order summer wear, to go shopping – even
buying mothballs was fun! – in a word, they were preparing for
departure from Moscow, for their holidays in country cottages,
in the Caucasus, in the Crimea and abroad, in general, for
summer, which always seems as if it is bound to be happy and
very long.

How many fine, delightful suitcases and brand-new, creaky
baskets were bought then on Leont'ev Street and at Muir-
Merrilees'! How many people were shaved and shorn at
Basile's and Théodore's! And one after the other came sunny
exciting days, days with new smells, with newly clean streets,
with church cupolas newly brilliant against the clear sky, with a
new Strastnoy, with a new Petrovka, with new, bright dresses
on the smart ladies and beautiful women rushing along the
Kuznetsky in smart cabs, with some famous actor's new pale-
grey hat also rushing past on 'pneumatics'. Everybody was
finishing a section of their former life, a life that had not been
right, not as it should have been, and for virtually all of
Moscow it was the eve of a new, almost certainly happy life –
this was especially true for me, much more than anybody else,
or so it seemed then. And nearer and nearer came the time for
me to leave 'The North Pole', to leave behind my student days
spent there, and from morning to night I was engaged in
bustling about, in travelling all over Moscow, absorbed in all
manner of happy preoccupations. And what was my room-
mate, our supremely modest contemporary, doing? Why,
roughly the same as the rest of us. At last what had happened
to us had happened to him too.

This passage describes the rapid revival of Moscow and its

inhabitants after a long, hard winter. Throughout the passage there is a sense of renewal and increasingly excited expectation. This unity of tone is conveyed very strongly through the language used: the use of such verbs as *менять или готовились изменить; зажить; близился и близился;* such adverbs as *как бы сначала; уже по-иному, чем прежде; весело; чуть не для всей;* such nouns and adjectives as *множество; к отъезду, к отдыху; чистотой; блеском; щеголихах и красавицах; счастливым и долгим, долгим; прекрасных, радующих, новеньких; новый* (eight times). The passage's tone also finds syntactic expression in the use of a fervent hypotaxis and piling up of elements.

Development proceeds from two initial, general and contrasting statements through an excited, cumulative catalogue of detail to a climax of two brief summary clauses. Within this overall framework the focus shifts from Moscow to its inhabitants, to a single inhabitant (the narrator) and finally to one more inhabitant, also infected by the 'Spring Fever'. In the same way a complex of imagery depicting people and things experiencing the Spring revival pervades the passage.

Throughout, the vocabulary used is simple, concrete, literal and highly sensuous, appealing very strongly to sight, sound and smell. It is aptly dominated by nouns denoting people, places and objects. There is a roughly equal use of adjectives conveying novelty and happiness, with fewer verbs and adverbs, yet these too convey images of change to a new, busy activity. Pronouns are not widely used but, when used, are used to great effect, e.g. *что-то* in the second sentence; *что же* in the antepenultimate, and the repeated *то же* of the last two sentences. None of the phraseology is striking in its originality but, rather, in the dynamic coupling of adjectives with nouns and adverbs with verbs to convey the feel of the 'Spring Fever'.

The extract begins with a deceptively simple sentence: its subject is Moscow, the whole city. The prefix *про-* on the verb emphasises the end of enduring and getting through a winter not only *утомительную* but also *сложную,* implying a multitude of difficulties. The long vowels to some extent contribute to this. The same verb is then extended to the next, much longer, sentence, thereby providing a link, but there is a change of verb, with the inceptive prefix *по-,* significantly after *Пасху,* implying a different kind of rebirth. There are similarly many implications in the use of *будто* as a subordinating conjunction and in the indefinite *что-то*. After *будто* there is an emphatic, virtual parallelism of three clauses, but the subtle placing of *чего-то настоящего* after the verb does create a strong sense of expectation.

The focus then shifts to the Muscovites themselves in the next immense clause, the cumulative rhythm of which effects a splendid build-up from the ripple of the first sentence and the ground-swell of the second. It is syntactically remarkable, since its six dozen words are subordinate to the first five, i.e. *И было множество москвичей, которые* (N.B. alliterations). The relative clause, beginning *которые . . .*, divides into the blunt *уже меняли* and the key concept *готовились*, paralleled by a further *готовились* and *спешили*, intimating the feverish activity of the second, major paragraph. Each of these verbs is used in a different way: *готовились* governs three infinitives, two of which are qualified by a series of adverbs emphasising change (N.B. the idiosyncratic use of *моложе*); *спешили* governs three phrases describing vernal activities (the seemingly innocent interpolation of *а ведь покупать (даже нафталин) весело!* implies that even such a banal activity as buying mothballs is special in the circumstances); the second *готовились* governs a string of nouns, where adverbs also play a subtly emphatic part, i.e. *одним словом; вообще; как всегда; непременно*, as does the joyful repetition of *долгим, долгим*.

The first half of the second paragraph effects a change of focus onto objects and frenetic activity by its being crowded with nouns and adjectives. This section is very reminiscent of paintings of Parisian crowd scenes in 'La Belle Epoque'. The very first sentence is instrumental in this: *сколько*, echoed in the second sentence, immediately emphasises great quantity, the adjectives greatly appeal to many senses (N.B. *скрипящих*), the passive usage – *было куплено* – and the absence of agent temporarily remove the human element, while the consonants *к/р/н* accommodate sound to sense. Throughout this paragraph the names of shops and streets impart a vivid reality to the scene. The paratactic linkage of the passive verbs *стриглось* and *брилось* both emphasises the activities while retaining the impersonality. The next long sentence also has a non-human subject – *дни*, although the string of dependent prepositional phrases extends both to people and objects, sights, sounds and smells. The heart of the extract is here with its *один за другим*, multiple repetition of *новый* and finely observed, seemingly insignificant detail, e.g. the colour of the famous actor's hat.

The second half of this paragraph, through generalisation, narrows the focus down to one inhabitant of Moscow, the narrator. The universality of the revival is conveyed by two clauses beginning *все кончали* and *чуть не для всей Москвы* and what it promises by the repetition of the verbs *близился и близился* and a series of prepositional phrases using the by now highly exploited *с* i.e. *разлуки с 'Северным полюсом'; со всем тем; был я в хлопотах, в разъездах; во всяческих радостных заботах.*

The hectic bustle of the passage ends quietly with three, appropriately brief, paratactic clauses extending these activities to his *скромнейший современник*. The first two clauses are carefully balanced by the final placing of their grammatical subjects. The final clause skilfully sums up everything by the syntactic device of beginning *с ним* and ending *со всеми нами*.

АЛЕКСА́НДР АЛЕКСА́НДРОВИЧ БЛОК

(1880–1921)

Brought up in St Petersburg almost entirely among women (his mother fled from her violent husband back to her father) – his mother, aunts and grandmother – music and literature, he grew to be a mystic worshipper of the Ideal Feminine with a pathologically reserved, ambisexual personality. In 1897 he made a trip to Germany and experienced his first love. At university he read Law up to 1901, then Philology to 1906. His first poetry, 'Ante Lucem' (1898–1900) and *Стихи́ о Прекра́сной Да́ме* (1901–2), proclaims the worship of the 'Beautiful Lady' – a combination of his wife-to-be, Solov'yov's 'Eternal Feminine', music, Russia and an hallucination. These were the years of his passionate love for L. D. Mendeleyeva, the great chemist's daughter, whom he married in 1903. They were also the years he lived among bohemian Symbolist circles and, as Zamyatin later cynically commented, 'persistently tried to turn water into wine', i.e. his symbolist poetry was a way of sublimating repressed eroticism and compulsive drinking. Significantly, after his marriage the 'Beautiful Lady' gradually turned into an unidentified whore.

Though quite apolitical and too romantic ever to be intellectually capable of understanding historical processes, Blok joined Gor'ky and hailed the 1905 Revolution, but fell into despair after its failure. In 1916 he served behind the lines and did various jobs for the Provisional Government in 1917. After the Bolshevik Revolution he did translation work, wrote journalistic articles and gave recitations. He died in 1921 after a heart-attack which doctors had initially diagnosed as merely another psychosomatic illness. His intense, complex poetic development culminated in *Двена́дцать* (1918), a narrative poem in a variety of idioms dominated by the figure of an ambiguous Christ.

Художник

(1913)

В жаркое лето и в зиму метельную,
В дни ваших свадеб, торжеств, похорон,
Жду, чтоб спугнул мою скуку смертельную
4.   Лёгкий, доселе неслышанный звон.

Вот он – возник. И с холодным вниманием
Жду, чтоб понять, закрепить и убить.
И перед зорким моим ожиданием
8.   Тянет он еле приметную нить.

С моря ли вихрь? Или сирины райские
В листьях поют? Или время стоит?
Или осыпали яблони майские
12.   Снежный свой свет? Или ангел летит?

Длятся часы, мировое несущие.
Ширятся звуки, движенье и свет.
Прошлое страстно глядится в грядущее.
16.   Нет настоящего. Жалкого нет.

И, наконец, у предела зачатия
Новой души, неизведанных сил, –
Душу сражает, как громом, проклятие:
20.   Творческий разум усилил – убил.

И замыкаю я в клетку холодную
Лёгкую, добрую птицу свободную,
Птицу, хотевшую смерть унести,
24.   Птицу, летевшую душу спасти.

Вот моя клетка – стальная, тяжёлая,
Как золотая, в вечернем огне.
Вот моя птица, когда-то весёлая,
28.   Обруч катает, поёт на окне.

Крылья подрезаны, песни заучены.
Любите вы под окном постоять?
Песни вам нравятся. Я же, измученный,
32.   Нового жду – и скучаю опять.

The Artist

In summer heat or winter snows,
On days of weddings, festivities, funerals,
I await the scaring off of my terrible boredom
By a faint, hitherto unheard ringing.

And here it is. And with chill attention
I wait to understand, fasten and kill it.
And before my vigilant expectation
It draws an almost invisible thread.

Is it a tornado from the sea? Or heavenly sirens
Singing among the leaves? Or has time stopped?
Or have May apple-trees strewn
Their snowy light? Or did an angel pass?

The mundane hours last and last,
Sound, movement and light expand.
The past peers passionately into the future.
There is no present, nothing pitiable.

And at last on the point of conceiving
A new spirit, unexperienced powers, –
The spirit is thunder-struck, felled by a curse:
It is overwhelmed and killed by creative intellect.

And in a chill cage I close up
The delicate, kind and free bird,
The bird which wanted to bear death away,
The bird which came to save a spirit.

Here is my cage – of steel, and heavy
As gold, in the evening light.
Here is my once happy bird,
Rolling a hoop, singing at the window.

Its wings are clipped, its songs are stale.
Do you like standing by the window?
You like the songs, but I, exhausted,
And bored again, wait for something new.

In this poem Blok is attempting to convey the difficult, almost
ineffable, process of the generation of a poem, the written,

finished work symbolised by a caged bird. With the stages of the process the authorial tone changes from an initially bored but expectant dissatisfaction – *скуку смертельную* – to a predatory alertness – *с холодным вниманием убить; зорким моим ожиданием* – to a tense, timeless expectation – *нет настоящего* – to an almost callous triumph – *клетку холодную; стальная, тяжёлая* – back to an exhausted, yet expectant dissatisfaction – *когда-то весёлая; подрезаны, песни заучены; я же, измученный; скучаю.* The poem follows a distinct, but subtle development, each stanza tightly encapsulated by alternating feminine and masculine rhymes, marking a stage (q.v. infra) in the process. The verse is written in an expressively flexible, but never 'sing-song', dactylic metre.

The poem's relatively simple vocabulary comprehends both the concrete and the abstract, the intellectual and the sensuous, appealing especially to the ear. Likewise, the images of the poem embrace the outer world of Man and Nature: *лето; зима; свадьба; похороны; вихрь; яблони; птица* and the inner world of the artist's emotions, e.g. *скука; внимание; ожидание; измученный.* Despite its conveying a process the poem is dominated by nouns, imparting to the process a static, meditative quality. While a wide and interesting variety of adjectives and verbs is used, only a handful of adverbs is used, thereby playing down the impact of the verbs. The relatively simple vocabulary is combined into an often striking and effective phraseology, e.g. *доселе неслышанный звон; с холодным вниманием; снежный свой свет; ширятся звуки; разум убил.*

The second half of the first stanza depicts the poet in a mood of bored but expectant dissatisfaction, contrasting with the normal and antithesised passage of the seasons and normal human events in the first half – consider the contrast of *ваших/мою.* However, all this is seen as a total situation since the stanza is a single syntactical unit. The end-stopping of the first two lines draws attention to events in the outside world, while metre and rhythm emphasise each item (N.B. the use of the plural in the second line). Attention is drawn to *жду* by a comma creating tension within the metre, while the alliterated *с/у* match sound to mood. The striking use, reminiscent of Rilke, of the half-personified auditory image *звон* to convey the beginning of the process of generation is emphasised by its final placing by means of syntactical inversion, by rhyme and by the break in the metre to highlight *лёгкий*, while the alliterated *с/з* unify *доселе неслышанный звон.*

The artist's mood changes abruptly in the second stanza to one of an almost predatory alertness with the unexpected blend of *понять* and *убить.* Counterpointed rhythm and metre are employed to vigorous effect in the first two lines. The metre stresses *вот*, while the interruption effected by the dash and the first stress of the next foot, itself interrupted by a full-stop, strongly emphasises *возник*, a verb very much restricted to abstract ideas. After the striking phrase *с холодным вниманием* with its interplay of *в/н/м/о*, one is stopped, as in l.3, by the abrupt *жду* and similarly *понять.* The metrical and rhythmic emphasis on *закрепить и убить* cannot but draw attention to this unusual and deliberately mixed metaphor. The two halves of this stanza are decisively separated by their being two separate syntactical units. The disposition of metric emphasis picks out the unusual coupling of *зорким . . . ожиданием.* One is perhaps reminded of the nature of the 'prey' by the auditory echoing of phrases in ll.4 and 8: *доселе неслышанный . . . еле приметную.*

A mood of impersonal uncertainty and almost of confusion appears in stanza 3 in the artist's attempt to ascertain, by five quite contrasting images, what it is he seeks. Rhythm and metre play a considerable part in conveying this uncertainty. The abrupt interrogative in the middle of the second foot draws attention to the first possibility – *вихрь* – a violent auditory image. Rhythm, metre and enjambement combine to delineate the second possibility, a totally different auditory image, appropriately containing the liquids *л/р.* His feeling of complete uncertainty is well conveyed by the desperately brief question – *или время стоит?* The fourth, visual variant, depicted as a delicate shower of petalled light, is expressively conveyed by metre/rhythm accord, enjambement and the alliterated *с.* The final possibility is expressed in the same manner as in l.10, implying both uncertainty and the uniqueness of the occasion.

The fourth stanza retains the impersonality of the preceding one in its conveying the artist's heightened perception of space and time. As in stanza 3, but entirely differently, the rhythm and structure of the verse combine to emphasise his changed perceptions. Changes in his perception of time are highlighted by a completely end-stopped initial line (the only one except in the last stanza). Syntactic inversion and metre immediately emphasise these apparent time-distortions. The same device is extended to the completely end-stopped second line, but this time the position-stressed verb *ширятся* is unexpectedly ascribed to sound, movement and light simultaneously. Yet another fully end-stopped line makes ll.13–15 unique in the poem, bringing them very boldly into relief. Line 15, however, differs from the other two in fluidity of movement and sound, appropriately conveying the artist's perception of past and future. The chiasmic inversions of l.6, stressed by metre and caesura, give a dogmatic assurance to his assertions concerning the loss of a sense of the present and any feelings of compassion.

The climax, 'the kill', is introduced by the metrically stressed *и* and *наконец* (also followed by a comma). In the first half the artist is on the point of witnessing the conception of the potentially prodigious child of his imagination, whose qualities are emphasised by enjambement, metre and alliteration – consider the impact of *неизведанных*. However, rhyme – *сил/убил* – compels us to contemplate the paradoxical tragedy – *проклятие* – of its conception: to 'live' in the world it must be 'killed' (given rational, organised form) by reason. The vocabulary is appropriately heightened at this point: *душа; проклятие; сражать*. The broken rhythm of l.19 emphasises *громом*, while *проклятие* receives emphasis from position, the half-rhyme with *зачатия* and guttural alliteration *г/к*. Rationality's Pyrrhic victory is conveyed by the confident movement of l.20 suddenly being broken up by the dash before the unexpected yet euphonic *убил*.

In contrast with the four preceding stanzas, the sixth stanza is a complete syntactical unit giving a self-contained finality to the artist's callous act, effectively disposing of his creation by contrasting *замыкаю я в клетку холодную* (N.B. alliteration) with the thrice repeated *птицу* and its attributes *лёгкую; добрую ... свободную. Лёгкую* is emphasised by its being the rejet of l.22, and the line as a whole by its metric and vocalic fluidity. The remarkable potential of *птица* (N.B. position) is stressed by identical syntax and almost identical rhythm.

The penultimate stanza draws attention by antithesis to the fate of the 'bird'. The *вот* of l.25 points to the cage, and caesura and punctuation stress its unpleasant qualities, whereas the *вот* of l.27 points to the fate of the bird, again highlighted by caesuras, *обруч* symbolising the tedium of its 'existence'.

In the final stanza the wheel has turned full circle – the final rhymed *опять* strongly emphasising the return of his initial mood of expectant dissatisfaction. This stanza operates in contrasts: the two end-stopped lines 29 and 30 boldly present the forlorn 'bird' for an imaginary spectator. The caesura of l.31 contrasts the smooth rhythm of the initial two feet with the broken *я же, измученный*, with its ironic half-rhyme. The final line re-presents the original situation entirely, by falling into two parts: expectation conveyed by the positionally stressed *нового* and the repeated *жду*, and dissatisfaction by the verbal equivalent – *скучаю* – of the noun in l.3.

АНДРЕЙ БЕЛЫЙ

(1880–1934)

Born in Moscow in 1880 Boris N. Bugaev, who later wrote under the name Andrei Bely, was the son of a Professor of Mathematics. He studied mathematics, zoology and philosophy at Moscow University, while maintaining an interest in art and mysticism. Like Blok (q.v.) he was influenced by the poetry and philosophy of Solov'yov, and became one of the most influential writers of the 1920s, although largely ignored by the Bolsheviks.

He became known first of all for a story in poetic prose, *Симфония* (1902). He collaborated with Bryusov (q.v.) in the publication of the Symbolist journal, *Весы*, from 1904 to 1909, and his subtle and sophisticated criticism gave the Symbolist movement a real theoretical basis, especially *Символизм*. In 1914 he joined a Rudolph Steiner anthroposophical community in Switzerland. His chief works belong to this period, especially *Петербург* (1913–16) which, in the tradition of Gogol' and Doestoevsky, presents the city as a spectrally beautiful, murderous, haunted place in a uniquely sophisticated, complex prose. His finest work in rhythmical prose, *Серебряный голубь*, dates back to 1909. His other chief work is *Котик Летаев*, the 'Ulysses' of an infant's coming to awareness.

He returned to Russia in 1916 and at first welcomed the Bolshevik Revolution. After a variety of confused literary activities he emigrated in 1921 but returned, disillusioned with the West, in 1923. An important, but less well-known part of his work, belongs to this period: his memoirs, his *Воспоминания о Блоке* (1922) and the semi-autobiographical trilogy, *На рубеже двух столетий* (1930), *Начало века* (1933) and *Между двух революций* (1934). In his last years he was published in small editions and largely ignored, although his influence on writers like Zamyatin, Pil′nyak (qq.v.), Fedin and Leonov was immense.

Петербург

(1916)

Изморось поливала улицы и проспекты, тротуары и крыши; низвергалась холодными струйками с жестяных жёлобов.

Изморось поливала прохожих: награждала их гриппами; вместе с тонкою пылью дождя инфлюэнзы и гриппы заползали под приподнятый воротник: гимназиста, студента, чиновника, офицера, субъекта, и субъект (так сказать, обыватель) озирался тоскливо; и глядел на проспект стёрто-серым лицом; циркулировал он в бесконечность проспектов, преодолевал бесконечность, без всякого ропота – в бесконечном токе таких же, как он – среди лёта, грохота, трепетанья пролёток, слушал издали мелодичный голос автомобильных рулад и нарастающий гул жёлто-красных трамваев (гул потом убывающий снова) в непрерывном окрике голосистых газетчиков.

Из одной бесконечности убегал он в другую; и потом, спотыкался о набережную; здесь приканчивалось всё: мелодичный глас автомобильной рулады, жёлто-красный трамвай и всевозможный субъект; здесь был и край земли, и конец бесконечностям.

А там-то, там-то: глубина, зеленоватая муть; издалека-далека, будто дальше, чем следует, опустились испуганно и принизились острова; принизились земли; и принизились здания; казалось – опустятся воды, и хлынет на них в этот миг: глубина, зеленоватая муть; а над этою зеленоватою мутью в тумане гремел и дрожал, вон туда убегая, чёрный, чёрный такой Николаевский мост.

В это хмурое петербургское утро распахнулись тяжёлые двери роскошного жёлтого дома: жёлтый дом окнами выходил на Неву. Бритый лакей с золотым галуном на отворотах бросился из передней подавать знаки кучеру. Серые в яблоках кони рванулись к подъезду; подкатили карету, на которой был выведен стародворянский герб: единорог, прободающий рыцаря.

Молодцеватый квартальный, проходивший мимо крыльца, поглупел и вытянулся в струну, когда Аполлон Аполлонович Аблеухов в сером пальто и в высоком чёрном цилиндре с каменным лицом, напоминающим пресс-папье, быстро выбежал из подъезда и ещё быстрее вбежал на подножку кареты, на ходу надевая чёрную замшевую перчатку.

Аполлон Аполлонович Аблеухов бросил мгновенный, растерянный взгляд на квартального надзирателя, на карету, на кучера, на большой чёрный мост, на пространство Невы, где так блёкло чертились туманные, многотрубные дали, и откуда испуганно поглядел Васильевский остров.

Серый лакей поспешно хлопнул каретною дверцею. Карета стремительно пролетела в туман, и случайный квартальный, потрясённый всем виденным, долго-долго глядел чрез плечо в грязноватый туман – туда, куда стремительно пролетела карета; и вздохнул, и пошёл; скоро скрылось в тумане и это плечо квартального, как скрывались в тумане все плечи, все спины, все серые лица и все чёрные, мокрые зонты. Посмотрел туда же и почтенный лакей, посмотрел направо, налево, на мост, на пространство Невы, где так блёкло чертились туманные, многотрубные дали, и откуда испуганно поглядел Васильевский остров.

Drizzle watered the streets and avenues, pavements and roofs; it came crashing down in cold streams from tin gutters.

Drizzle watered passers-by: it rewarded them with 'flu; along with a fine spray of rain, influenzas and 'flus crept under upturned collars: the school-boy's, the student's, the officer's, the character's and the character (a resident, so to speak) looked round miserably; with a worn grey face he looked at the avenue; circulated in an infinity of avenues, overcame the infinity, and without complaining – in an endless stream of people just like him – amid the flying, crashing and flickering of cabs, from the distance he listened to the musical voice of motor roulades and the growing rumble of yellowish-red trams (the rumble dying away again later) amid the incessant shouting of loud-voiced paper-boys.

From one infinity he fled to another; and then he stumbled upon the embankment; everything came to an end here: the musical locution of motor roulades, the yellowish-red tram and the multifarious character; here too was the edge of the land and an end to infinities.

And out there, out there: depth, greenish murk; and far, far away, seeming farther than they ought, the islands sank, submissive and fearful; land sank in submission; buildings sank submission, it seemed that the waters would go down, and over them at that moment would pour depth, greenish murk; and above this greenish murk, rumbling and trembling in the mist, rushing away over there was the black, so black, Nicholas Bridge.

On this gloomy Petersburg morning the heavy doors of a splendid yellow house were flung open: the windows of the yellow house looked out on the Neva. A clean-shaven footman with gold braid on his lapels rushed from the lobby to give signals to the coachman. Dapple-grey steeds darted to the porch, bringing with them a carriage on which was drawn the old family crest: a unicorn goring a knight.

A sprightly policeman, passing the porch, went stupid and stood to attention when Apollon Apollonovich Ableukhov in a grey overcoat and tall black top-hat, with a stony, blotting-paper face, quickly ran from the porch and even more quickly ran onto the footboard of the carriage, putting on a black suede glove en route.

Apollon Apollonovich Ableukhov cast a momentary look of dismay at the policeman, the carriage, the big black bridge, the expanse of the Neva, where so wanly outlined were misty, many-chimneyed distant prospects, and from where Vasil'evsky Island glanced in fear.

The grey footman hastily slammed the carriage-door. The carriage sped off into the mist, and the fortuitous policeman, stunned by all he'd seen, looked over his shoulder for a long, long time into the dirty mist to where the carriage had sped, sighed and went on his way; this policeman's shoulder was soon swallowed up in the mist, as are all shoulders, all backs, all grey faces and all black, wet umbrellas. The venerable footman also looked in the same direction, to the right, to the left, at the bridge, at the expanse of the Neva, where so wanly outlined were misty, many-chimneyed distant prospects, and from where Vasil'evsky Island glanced in fear.

In this excerpt from the novel we are given a description of Ableukhov's hasty morning departure in the mysterious gloom of Petersburg. Over the whole passage a complex, almost indefinable, disconsolate uncertainty hangs like a sodden blanket. This feeling is partly conveyed by diction: *изморось; заползала; тоскливо; испуганно; серый; туманный; чёрные;*

мокрые; partly by syntax – the use of parallelism extends the foul weather over everything: *улицы и проспекты, тротуары и крыши*; repetition conveys the inhuman uncertainty of the city: *циркулировал он в бесконечность; преодолевал бесконечность; в бесконечном токе*; paratactic lists extend the mood of the city to all, irrespective of status: *гимназиста, студента, чиновника, офицера, субъекта; все плечи, все спины, все серые лица и все чёрные, мокрые зонты.*

The passage falls into two parts, according to its focus: Petersburg and the 'character'; Petersburg and Ableukhov. The pattern of presentation is different in each part. In the first part a narrowing of focus rather than a sequence of events is apparent: from the weather to the 'character' as its victim, his uncertain movements within it, ending with a vision of the Neva. Virtually all of this section is narrated in the imperfective aspect, thus emphasising a state rather than a sequence of events. In the second half a perfective narrative sequence is followed, until the carriage dissolves, along with everything else, into the mist. This half, like the first, ends with a vision of the Neva. However, unity is maintained through tone and subject-matter: the eerie presence of Petersburg seems to hang over everything. Part of the impact of this extract lies in its images and the vision they convey of this strange city, e.g. the climate: *изморось; инфлюэнзы и гриппы; в тумане; хмурое петербургское утро; чёрные, мокрые зонты*; the city and the river: *бесконечность проспектов; зеленоватая муть; опустились испуганно и принизились острова; испуганно поглядел Васильевский остров*; its people and their activities: *в бесконечном токе; среди лёта, грохота, трепетанья пролёток, слушал издали мелодичный голос автомобильных рулад и нарастающий гул жёлто-красных трамваев (гул потом убывающий снова) в непрерывном окрике голосистых газетчиков; стёрто-серым лицом; с каменным лицом, напоминающим пресс-папье.* A very strongly visual, elaborate vocabulary is employed to convey and emphasise the visionary nature of the city, although there are ephemeral references to city sounds, which are soon absorbed by the atmosphere. Moreover, apart from Apollon Apollonovich Ableukhov's departure, where verbs conveying swift movement follow in rapid succession, this vision of Petersburg is a static one of nouns and adjectives. Adverbs are used infrequently but graphically, e.g. *тоскливо; испуганно; блёкло.* Bely's originality is most evident in the passage's striking and idiosyncratic phraseology, e.g. *изморось . . . низвергалась; награждала их гриппами; инфлюэнзы и гриппы заползали; бесконечность проспектов; принизились острова; испуганно поглядел Васильевский остров.*

Petersburg's climate makes itself felt from the very first word of the passage, especially its effect with the vivid, if idiosyncratic, use of *поливала.* Surfaces, set in co-ordinated parallel, receive the drizzle – Bely's strongly visual imagination is evident here. *Низвергалась* at first seems bizarre with reference to drizzle, until elucidation is provided at the end of the sentence, intimating the sheer volume of precipitation, its unpleasantness conveyed by the one adjective – *холодным* – and its force by the dactylic rhythms of the adjective and noun combinations. The first two sentences are held in abrupt parataxis and, in forming an introductory paragraph, set in relief a dismal scene.

The effects of the climate extend to the city's inhabitants: the passage's initial sentence is paralleled by the telegraphic statement *изморось поливала прохожих* maintaining a deliberate impersonality in the use of *прохожих* who suffer by the grotesque irony of the 'reward': *награждала их гриппами.* To achieve variety the drizzle is now referred to metaphorically, while the deleterious effects of this climate are strikingly conveyed by the personification *инфлюэнзы и гриппы заползали.* The movement of the sentence is temporarily stopped by a colon to allow contemplation of the subsequent list and its implied universality, extending to the mysterious *субъект*, his status questioned by the parenthesis. By a sudden and abrupt switch, effected by a startling repetition, the 'character' becomes the centre of attention, and by a play on words the perceiving subject of the Petersburg phantasm. His perception of Petersburg accords with the weather – *тоскливо*; his activities deliberately generalised – *озирался; глядел; циркулировал; преодолевал; слушал* and almost mechanised by the absence of co-ordination.

To maintain unity of effect Bely employs a form of synecdoche (typical of Modernist prose) by having the *face* look, thereby allowing him to employ the disconsolate *стёрто-серым.* Difficulty of movement in the city is strikingly conveyed by the weighty and evocative *циркулировал он в бесконечность*, and the transference of noun into adjective in *в бесконечном токе*. The impersonality of this activity is conveyed by *таких же, как он*. At this point the sounds of the city intrude and blend in a confusing synaesthesia: *среди лёта; грохота; трепетанья пролёток* and the whole section from *мелодичный* to *газетчиков*, where the effect is heightened by word rhythm and the alliterated *т/л/р/г*. Extensive use of parataxis and the consequent stuttering phrase rhythms in this paragraph heighten the vividness of a series of strange, flashed images. Moreover, by rhythmic contrast the last clause comes into prominence against the previous staccato ones, emphasising the noise and activity at the heart of the city.

The accumulated impressions of the second paragraph serve to emphasise the events of the brief third one, where *приканчивалось* (an unexpected verb) *всё*, including the puzzling but elusively suggestive *всевозможный субъект*. The sudden appearance of the Neva is vividly expressed by *спотыкался о набережную*. The strange finality of this water barrier is conveyed by the striking contradiction *конец бесконечностям* and word-order.

The spectral quality of the Neva is presented by the skilful employment of a number of linguistic resources: the alarmed repetition of the emphatic *там-то*; the nature of the river expanse: not water but *глубина, зеленоватая муть*; the expression of the improbable distance of the islands by repetition and qualification; the sense of the impending fearful possibility of a murky deluge by the personification and repetition of *опустились испуганно и принизились острова; принизились земли; и принизились здания*. The air of terrifying unreality is heightened by the one recognisable landmark, the Nicholas Bridge, being depicted in terms of a black noise shrouded in mist. The appropriately disjointed rhythms of this paragraph are effected by punctuation and co-ordination being limited to *и* and *а*.

The second, partially narrative, section presents a strong contrast in its greater visual precision and sense of purposeful activity through a series of perfective verbs conveying brisk movement. This large, splendid building, like the nameless and transient 'character' of the first section, looks out on the Neva. The paragraph begins with a strong, sudden contrast of purposeful activity and colour: *распахнулись; бросился; рванулись;*

подкатили; жёлтый; бритый; золотым. Use of clause parataxis in this paragraph accelerates the activities described, because the rhythm is not broken up by punctuation. A Gogolesque series of details ensues, despite the continuation of the feverish activity. Although Ableukhov's importance had been intimated by details indicating considerable wealth, at this point it is expressed by the grotesque *поглупел и вытянулся в струну.* Like the now forgotten 'character', Ableukhov matches his Petersburg environment: *в сером пальто и в высоком чёрном цилиндре с каменным лицом, напоминающим пресс-папье.*

The presence of Petersburg is again felt as Ableukhov's dismayed look quickly scans the scene, finally resting on the *пространство Невы,* the last adverb of the paragraph echoing the fearful intimations of an earlier paragraph. The effect of this long, cumulative sentence is momentarily to reassert the presence of the Neva. The final paragraph completely reasserts the primacy of the city and its climate. At first the camera as it were resumes the film, emphasised by the adverbs *поспешно* and the repeated *стремительно,* and the repetition of the simple conjunction *и.* The pace slows abruptly and a monochrome impersonality reasserts itself as everything dissolves in the mist, effected by the aspectical shift *скрылось/скрывались,* and the assertive repetition of *все.* Ultimately, as at the end of the first section, the river remains the dominant image, especially because of the long and emphatic, identical repetition.

МАРИ́НА ИВА́НОВНА ЦВЕТА́ЕВА

(1892–1941)

Her father was a professor of Art History in Moscow where she was born, while her mother was of working-class origin. She began writing in 1898 (sic!) and published her first volume of poetry, *Вечéрний альбóм* in 1910, which received a certain amount of favourable acclaim. Despite a number of esoteric influences, especially French poetry, her own poetry was a very complex 'confessional' poetry, capricious and violently passionate.

She travelled widely in Europe, studied at the Sorbonne and completely rejected the Bolshevik Revolution, staunchly supporting her husband, S. Efron, who fought for the Whites in the Civil War. In 1922 she was allowed to emigrate, but found reactionary émigré circles as unacceptable as the Bolsheviks. After years of wandering, desperate poverty and estrangement from émigré circles she returned to the Soviet Union in 1939 where, after the tragic loss of her family during the early days of the German invasion, she hanged herself in 1941. Increasingly acceptable in the Soviet Union since the sixties, she is now ranked with Akhmatova as a major twentieth-century Russian poetess.

Попытка ревности

(1924)

Как живётся вам с другою, –
Проще ведь? – Удар весла! –
Линией береговою
Скоро ль память отошла

4.

Обо мне, пловучем острове
(По́ небу – не по водам!)
Ду́ши, ду́ши! быть вам сёстрами,
8.   Не любовницам – вам!

Как живётся вам с *простою*
Женщиною? *Без* божеств?
Государыню с престола
12.   Свергши (с оного сошед),

Как живётся вам – хлопочется –
Ёжится? Встаётся – как?
С пошлиной бессмертной пошлости
16.   Как справляетесь, бедняк?

'Судорог да перебоев –
Хватит! Дом себе найму.'
Как живётся вам с любою –
20.   Избранному моему!

Свойственнее и съедобнее –
Снедь? Приестся – не пеняй . . .
Как живётся вам с подобием –
24.   Вам, поправшему Синай!

Как живётся вам с чужою,
Здешнею? Ребром –люба?
Стыд Зевесовой вожжою
28.   Не охлёстывает лба?

Как живётся вам – здоровится –
Можется? Поётся – как?
С язвою бессмертной совести
32.   Как справляетесь, бедняк?

Как живётся вам с товаром
Рыночным? Оброк – крутой?
После мраморов Каррары
36.   Как живётся вам с трухой

Гипсовой? (Из глыбы высечен
Бог – и начисто разбит!)
Как живётся вам с стотысячной –
40.   Вам, познавшему Лилит!

Рыночною новизною
Сыты ли? К волшбам остыв,
Как живётся вам с земною

44.   Женщиною, *без* шестых

Чувств? Ну, за́ голову: счастливы?
Нет? В провале без глубин –
Как живётся, милый? Тяжче ли,

48.   Так же ли как мне с другим?

An Attempt at Jealousy

What's life like with another woman, –
Simpler, isn't it? – A stroke of the oar! –
Like a coastline
Did the memory of me soon recede,

Of me, a floating island.
(In the sky – not on the waters!)
My dears, my dears! You are to be sisters,
Not lovers, you two!

What's it like living with an *ordinary*
Woman? *Without* divine beings?
Having dethroned the queen
(And renounced the throne yourself),

How is life – are you busy –
Do you shiver? Getting up – what's it like?
Poor thing, how do you manage
The cost of immortal triviality?

'I've had enough of your spasms
And palpitations! I'll rent a house.'
What's life like with any old thing
For you, my chosen one!

Are the victuals more congenial
And edible? If it palls – don't complain . . .
What's life like with an image –
For you who have trodden Sinai?

What's life like with a stranger,
A mere mortal? Out with it – do you like her?
Does shame, like Zeus' reins,
Not lash your brow?

What's your life like – are you well –
How are things? Do you feel like singing?
Poor thing, how do you manage
A festering, immortal conscience?

What's life like with something bought
At the market? Is the price steep?
After Carrara marble
What's your life like with a lump

Of plaster? (God was carved
From a block – and has been smashed to pieces!)
What's your life like with one of the crowd –
You who have known Lilith!

Have you had enough of your market
Novelty? Bored with magic,
What's life like with an earthly
Woman, with ordinary senses?

Well, honestly, are you happy?
No? In a bottomless pit –
What's life like, my love? Is it harder,
Just as it is for me with another man?

The title understates the content and the theme: the poetess is
very jealous and angry, yet feigning partial concern and contempt, while her 'attempt' in poem form is in fact a brilliant
verbal annihilation of her rival. Thus the tone of the poem is a
subtle mixture of the said and the unsaid: a blend of feigned
bonhommie and concern for her ex-lover, immense contempt
for her mediocre rival, and scarcely concealed jealousy, rage
and offended pride. All these powerful feelings are revealed or
implied at various points in the poem. Her ostensible attitude
towards her lover in such expressions as: *проще ведь?; как
живётся вам; свойственнее и съедобнее – снедь?; бедняк;
поётся – как?*; towards her rival: *с простою женщиною; с*

пошлиной бессмертной пошлости; с подобием; с товаром рыночным; с трухой гипсовой; her jealousy, rage and offended pride: *вам; государыню с престола свергши; избранному моему; Синай; ребром – люба?; с язвою бессмертной совести.*

The poem has no development as such, consisting rather of the twelve-fold re-iteration of the same rhetorical question: *как живётся?,* and a series of answers expressing her complex feelings. Although the quatrain form with its subtle blend of masculine, feminine, dactylic full- and truncated rhymes controls the rhetorical questions, her feelings are so strong that they burst out of this framework and disregard the form, thus skilfully yet naturally combining powerful feeling with disciplined form. With equal skill she blends the potentially tedious trochee with a colloquial speaking voice, employing the counterpoint of metrical and rhythmic stresses for further effects.

The poem's imagery operates in terms of contrasts, especially upward and downward comparisons – references to herself are conveyed by the elevated, the superior, the unusual, e.g. *пловучем острове (по небу – не по водам!); государыню; Синай; мраморов Каррары; Лилит; волшбы;* references to 'her' by the ordinary, inferior and cheap, e.g. *простою женщиною; подобием; здешнею; товаром рыночным; трухой гипсовой;* references to him by the pathetic and mundane, e.g. *бедняк; хлопочется; встаётся; справляетесь; приестся; сыты ли?.* These images are expressed in a wide range of vocabulary of all registers, yet essentially of the intellectual, since her feelings are expressed through ideas – one does not feel the presence of the material world, despite references to objects or activities in it. This is further apparent in the overwhelming predominance of nouns with fundamentally intellectual references. Adjectives are used sparingly, but often with crushing effectiveness in a striking phraseology, e.g. *с пошлиной бессмертной пошлости; с язвою бессмертной совести; с трухой гипсовой; с земною женщиною; в провале без глубин.*

The poem begins with the apparently innocuous rhetorical question which echoes a dozen times through it – *как живётся вам?* (N.B. the pronoun). The feelings implied by the particle *ведь* must range from gentle sarcasm to blinding jealousy. The pause effected by the dash forces a caesura into the metre and breaks the rhythm into that of the speaking voice, also drawing attention to *удар весла* – just like pushing a stick through water and what that implies for the other woman – which generates another set of images, wherein the poetess sees herself as an abandoned island – in the sky, she quickly adds! The rhyming of *весла/отошла* links the two ideas, yet does not impede the fluid movement of the verse into the next stanza nor the positional emphasis on *скоро* (her unexpressed concern). The parenthesised qualification of l.6 is again broken by an imposed caesura, thereby strongly contrasting the two ideas.

Unexpectedly, in mid-stanza, the direction of her thought changes – you and *she* will never be more than sisters, never real lovers. This she expresses by the repeated and metrically stressed condescending *души, души!*. The exclamation-mark acts as a caesura and also emphasises the subsequent metrically and rhythmically stressed *быть сёстрами*, a use of the infinitive which often implies inevitability. The impact of l.8 is strong because the normally unstressed particle *не* receives metric stress while *вам*, picked out by dash, exclamation-mark and rhyme is (probably deliberately) just a fading cadence.

The third stanza picks up the question of l.1, but with the devastating substitution of the rhyming *простою*, while *женщиною* is relegated to the *rejet* of the enjambement. Following this, the normally unstressed *без* becomes a strongly emphatic interrogative, while *божеств* cannot but parallel *женщиною*, although precisely the opposite in implication. The question is made even more forceful by the assonance of the *е*. By a form of association this leads the poetess to royal thoughts, presenting herself as a dethroned monarch – *государыню*, with emphasis carried through by enjambement to *свергши*, while parenthesis halts the sibilant/liquid flow of the verse to effect consideration of a similar loss in the stressed *с óного сошéд*. The appropriately lofty and archaic forms of these two lines contrast with the banalities of stanza 4, with which they form a continuous unit. Still bearing in mind what has been lost in stanza 3, the question is repeated – and answered in the hissing staccato rhythms of the banal *хлопочется – /Ёжится? Встаётся*. Metric stress, position and rhyme put into relief *как?* – and all that it implies. This is echoed in the pathetic *бедняк* of l.16, following the splendidly vituperative and musical *с пошлиной бессмертной пошлости/как справляетесь* ... i.e. how can you possibly manage to cope with *that*?

Stanza 5 recollects his complaints against her tantrums with the forcefully positioned *хватит!* and his decision to leave her. However, after a repetition of the question, rhyme picks up *найму* in the powerful and infinitely condescending *избранному моему* which gains its power from the complex assonance of seven vowels, the alliterated *м* and only two rhythmic stresses – on the first and last syllables – thus emphasising *her* possession of *him*. The two comparatives of l.21 appear momentarily to be a concession, except for the hissing derogatory archaism held until the beginning of l.22 – *снедь*, and the casual colloquialism of *приестся – не пеняй* ... with the metrically stressed *не* and the loud silence of the dots. The question is quickly reiterated in ll.23 and 24 through an ingenious metaphor – he, like Moses, had ascended Sinai in his former relationship with the poetess, but now he has to live with a mere *подобием*, a useless, graven image, while *вам* receives both metric and positional emphasis, i.e. how could *you* sink to this?!

Stanza 7 takes up the question again, doubly dismissing the rival as *чужою/здешнею* – both emphasised by position. However, the line is literally burst asunder by her jealousy – the colloquial *ребром – люба?* where both words are stressed by metre and punctuation. As if quickly regaining her composure, she expresses her injured pride in an almost comic eighteenth-century periphrasis, whereby both *стыд* and *не* are stressed, as is *лба* in rhyming with *люба*. Stanza 8 echoes the fourth stanza, albeit in a tone of concerned, colloquial familiarity. However, as in stanza 4, *как* is made to rhyme with *бедняк* after the spitting, sibilant rage of *с язвою бессмертной совести/как справляетесь*.

The question is asked again, three times, in the next three stanzas of sheer and brilliant vituperation. The positions and stress of the three words in l.34 give them maximum emphasis, especially the multi-layered *оброк*. Abuse reaches unprecedented heights in ll.35–7, descending from a reference to herself as highest grade marble to the metrically and positionally stressed *трухой* with the derogatory *гипсовой* trailing into the next stanza. In order not to lose the impact of the 'stone' metaphor, she pursues it into implying that he has committed some ultimate sacrilege akin to smashing a Michelangelo

marble sculpture, each word of l.38 being fully stressed, with
Бог receiving extra emphasis by position. The second half of
the stanza takes up an attitude similar to stanza 6 and uses
Biblical mythology in referring to the poetess as Lilith, the first
and evil wife of Adam, i.e. she may be wicked, but she is the
first. This follows on the dismissal of the 'other' as the
100,000th, her outrage expressed by the repeatedly stressed
зам.

In the penultimate stanza her rival is dismissed as some new
trivial thing recently bought and soon tired of – *сыты* being
held until l.42. By position and sound *к волшбам* forms a
strong contrast, while *новизною* is taken up by the rhyming
земною, echoing ll.9 and 10, with their implied mediocrity
trailing into the next stanza. In the final stanza the poetess
overcomes her negative feelings in order to ascertain whether
he is suffering as much as she. This is effected in several ways:
direct, colloquial language breaking up the metrical rhythm of
the verse, emphasis on significant words, e.g. *нет?; милый* (an
unexpected hint of tenderness); *тяжче; так же* and the dismal
imagery of *в провале без глубин*.

БОРИ́С АНДРÉЕВИЧ ПИЛЬНЯ́К

(1894–1938?)

Pil'nyak (the pseudonym of B. A. Vogau) had his first stories published in 1915, some of which were later incorporated in the book that brought him fame – *Гóлый год* (1922) – a highly original, stylistic equivalent of the state of total flux caused by the Revolution and Civil War. His unorthodox vision of this period was not popular with Soviet critics and two further stories, *Пóвесть о непогáшенной лунé* (1926) and *Крáсное дéрево* (1929), brought him into disgrace. His effort to rewrite *Крáсное дéрево* as a Five-Year Plan novel, re-titled *Вóлга впадáет в Каспи́йское мóре* (1930), was a political failure, as was an attack on the American way of life – *О-кей* (1932). He disappeared in the Purges and his books have only recently (1978) been republished in the Soviet Union. Unique in his stylistic vision of the historical events of the period, Pil'nyak was nevertheless influenced by Bely and Remizov (qq.v.). He in turn exerted great influence on young Soviet writers of the twenties, especially the Serapion Brothers, a group which included such writers as Zamyatin (q.v.), Shklovsky, Fedin, Kaverin and Zoshchenko.

Голый год

(1922)

Поезд № пятьдесят седьмой – смешанный – ползёт по чёрной степи.

Люди, человеческие ноги, руки, головы, животы, спины, человеческий навоз, – люди, обсыпанные вшами, как этими людьми теплушки. Люди, собравшиеся здесь и отстоявшие право ехать с величайшими кулачными усилиями, ибо там, в голодных губерниях, на каждой станции к теплушкам бросались десятки голодных людей и через головы, шеи, спины, ноги по людям лезли во внутрь, – их били, они били, срывая, сбрасывая уже едущих, и побоище продолжалось до тех пор, пока не трогался поезд, увозя тех, кто застрял, – а эти, вновь влезшие, готовились к новой драке на новой станции. Люди едут неделями. Все эти люди давно уже потеряли различие между ночью и днём, между грязью и чистотой, и научились спать сидя, стоя, вися. В теплушке вдоль и поперёк в несколько ярусов настланы нары и на нарах, под нарами, на полу, на полках, во всех щелях, сидя, стоя, лёжа, притихли люди, – чтобы шуметь на станции. Воздух в теплушке изгажен человеческими желудками и махоркой. Ночью в теплушке темно, двери и люки закрыты. В теплушке холодно, в щели дует ветер. Кто-то хрипит, кто-то чешется, теплушка скрипит, как старый рыдван. Двигаться в теплушке нельзя, ибо ноги одного лежат на груди другого, а третий заснул под ними, и его ноги стали у шеи первого. И всё же – двигаются . . . Человек, у которого, должно быть, изъедены лёгкие, инстинктивно жмётся к двери, и около него, отодвинув дверь, люди, мужчины и женщины, отправляют свои естественные потребности, свисая над ползущими шпалами или приседая, – человек изучил во всех подробностях, как это далают, – все по разному.

У человека, сгорающего последним румянцем чахотки, странны и спутанны ощущения. Мысли о стоицизме и честности, маленькая его комнатка, его брошюры и книги, голод, – всё отлетело куда-то к чёрту.

Train No. 57 – a passenger and goods train – is crawling across the black steppe.

People, people's legs, arms, heads, stomachs, backs, people's excrement, – people, crawling with lice, just as the heated goods-wagons are crawling with people. People who have gathered here and have defended their right to travel with great fisticuffs, for out there in the starving provinces at every small station dozens of starving people have rushed at the wagons and clambered inside over heads, necks, backs and legs – beaten and beating, dragging off and throwing off those already travelling, and the carnage lasted until the train moved off, carrying away those who had stayed on – and those who had got on again got ready for another fight at another station. People are travelling for weeks. All these people have long forgotten the difference between day and night, dirt and cleanliness, and have learned to sleep standing, sitting, hanging. In the wagon plank-beds have been laid in several tiers crosswise and lengthwise and on the plank-beds, under the plank-beds, on the floor, on shelves, in all the cracks, sitting, standing, lying, people are quiet – in order to make a din at the next station. The air in the wagon has been fouled with people's stomachs and strong tobacco. It is dark in the wagon at night, the doors and hatches are closed. It is cold in the wagon and the wind is blowing through the cracks. Someone snores, someone scratches, the wagon squeaks like an old carriage. It is impossible to move in the wagon, for one person's legs are lying on another's chest, while another has fallen asleep under them, and his legs are on the first person's neck. And yet – they are on the move . . . A person whose lungs are probably eaten away instinctively presses himself to the door, and next to him, with the door open, people, men and women, answer the call of nature hanging over the crawling sleepers or squatting – a person learns how this is done in all its detail – everybody differently.

A person burning with the last flush of consumption has strange and confused feelings. Thoughts of stoicism and honesty, his little room, his pamphlets and books, hunger – it has all gone to the devil.

The subject-matter of this passage is a striking description of a train crammed with refugees from the starving countryside. However, the theme underlying this is that of gross degradation, the degradation of people reduced to dire extremities. This highly evocative description is intended to arouse feelings of revulsion and horror. Its powerful tone is achieved through a careful choice of lurid detail, e.g. the indifferent mixing of aspects of the human body in an impersonal conglomeration: *Люди, человеческие ноги, руки, головы, животы, спины, человеческий навоз*, and a very skilful use of syntax, e.g. the terse chiasmus of *люди, обсыпанные вшами, как этими людьми теплушки*. It should be stressed, however, that the writer remains aloof from his material – pity and compassion are quite absent.

Pil'nyak's purpose is achieved by the relentless accumulation of horrible detail, culminating in a tersely generalised final paragraph. The structuring of this accumulation is quite remarkable. The scene is set with an isolated, laconic single sentence, then a multitude of particular details is hurled at the reader in one enormous paragraph, culminating in a final two-sentence paragraph containing the writer's conclusions. In the major paragraph the sentences are not connected in temporal order but are, rather, a kind of collage of images accumulating horror upon horror. However, within this collage the overall picture gradually narrows down to the inside of one particular, though typical, heated goods-wagon.

The imagery of this passage is exclusively that of impersonal human degradation, presented in a very simple, literal language of lurid, concrete detail, assailing all the senses, including smell. The writer's concentration on detail finds its equivalent in the prominence of nouns, especially the generalised *люди* and *человек*. Verbs are cluttered together to emphasise violent or grotesque activity. Adjectives are used very sparingly and then in such striking, ironic phrases as *с величайшими кулачными усилиями; человеческий* is used three times, thus depersonalising individuals and highlighting the degeneration of that quality. There are only *two* true adverbs in the whole passage – significantly *инстинктивно* and *по-разному* (with the implication of necessity being the mother of invention). Similarly, there is a very limited use of pronouns, viz. *их; кто-то; они; эти; все* – all of an impersonal, generalised nature. Pil′nyak's phraseology is sparing, but striking, especially his deliberate use of such ironic phrases as *с величайшими кулачными усилиями; отправляют свои естественные потребности; во всех подробностях.*

The passage begins with a remarkably laconic, isolated sentence, creating immediacy by its use of *ползёт.* Further emphasis is achieved by the use of alliteration, i.e. *с/п.* There is a dramatic plunge into the first 'sentence' of the main paragraph – a paratactic, verbless accumulation of nouns from which the individual is purposely excluded and reduced to *люди* and *человеческий.* Humanity is further reduced by the striking chiasmus of *люди, обсыпанные вшами, как этими людьми теплушки.* (Note how graphic the past participle is.) *Люди* is repeated three times in the first two sentences, thereby emphasising how multitudinous the refugees are. This initial sentence is separated from the third sentence (consisting of three words) by a huge periodic sentence which, however, lacks a main verb. In its context the phrase *с величайшими кулачными усилиями* can only be considered ironic, while the bookish *ибо* and *побоище* are almost grotesque. A remarkable rhythm results from the tremendous accumulation of nouns and verbs combined with the long expository section *люди, собравшиеся здесь и отстоявшие право ехать с величайшими кулачными усилиями, ибо там, в голодных губерниях, на каждой станции к теплушкам бросались десятки голодных людей и через головы, шеи, спины, ноги по людям лезли во внутрь* followed by the parallel paratactic *их били, они били, срывая, сбрасывая* ... The impact of this great block of words is further heightened by the subsequent laconic *Люди едут неделями.*

The *все эти* of the next sentence emphasises the universality of this degradation, and their condition is further emphasised by the parallel phrases *между ночью и днём, между грязью и чистотой* and the series of gerunds with their alliterative consonants and vowel repetition, viz. *сидя, стоя, вися.*

In the next sentence, as the focus narrows to a single wagon, there is a skilful accumulation to a climax with the simple conjunction *и* followed by a list of nouns and gerunds. Alliteration and vowel sounds are again used to re-inforce detail, i.e. *н/п* and the sibilants, and the vowel *а* of *в несколько ярусов настланы нары и на нарах, под нарами, на полу, на полках, во всех щелях, сидя, стоя, лёжа* ... The balanced contrast of *притихли ... шуметь* is supremely effective.

The sentence rhythm now changes markedly, as a series of short, paratactic sentences amplifies the details, conveying images of smell, sight and sound to assail the senses. The effect is one of horror and utter degradation. The conditions in this particular wagon are reduced to the biologically impersonal: *Воздух в теплушке изгажен человеческими желудками и махоркой.* Appalling conditions are conveyed with stenographic matter-of-factness: *Ночью в теплушке темно, двери и люки закрыты. В теплушке холодно, в щели дует ветер.* Thus Pil'nyak achieves emphasis by understatement (c.f. and contrast with Gogol'and Sholokhov). Equal emphasis is achieved by the staccato rhythm of *кто-то хрипит, кто-то чешется, теплушка скрипит, как старый рыдван* with its impersonal *кто-то* and the sound-play of *к/х/ш/с/т/р.*

The antithetical punning of *Двигаться в теплушке нельзя* ... and *И всё-же – двигаются* serves to redeem the grotesque physical confusion by implying that there is some value for the travellers in such privations. Human life is really reduced to its basics in the following two sentences by the balancing of *Человек, у которого, должно быть, изъедены лёгкие, инстинктивно жмётся к двери* ... with the highly alliterative *и около него, отодвинув дверь, люди, мужчины и женщины, отправляют свои естественные потребности, свисая над ползущими шпалами или приседая* ... The irony of *отправляют свои естественные потребности* is almost grotesque in the context of death and excrement. This huge paragraph ends with the brutal understatement of *человек изучил во всех подробностях, как это делают, – все по-разному.*

In the final paragraph Pil'nyak states how the approach of death, conveyed by a vivid image, reduces all ideals and feelings to nothing – possibly an implied comment on what followed the high aspirations of 1917.

ОСИП ЭМИ́ЛЬЕВИЧ МАНДЕЛЬШТА́М

(1891–1938?)

Born of Jewish parents, he grew up in St Petersburg, where he was educated, except for a period at Heidelberg University. In 1910 he became acquainted with the poet Gumilyov (q.v.) and became an active member of the 'Acmeist' school of poetry, which demanded a classical clarity in poetry in reaction to Symbolist vagueness. In all he published three volumes of verse, *Ка́мень* (1913), *Tristia* (1922) and *Стихотворе́ния* (1928), each of which shows the dichotomy which pervaded his poetry: his horrified fascination with the upheaval, destruction and tyranny of the Revolution, contrasting sharply with his ideal of classical antiquity which he hoped might one day pervade and civilise Russia. Between these two poles he displayed a poignant love for the ambivalence of St Petersburg, a city at once classical yet insubstantial, whose destruction he witnessed. He also published a number of prose works, viz. *О поэ́зии* (1928), *Еги́петская ма́рка* (1928) and *Четвёртая проза* (1930).

His persecution by the Soviet authorities for ideological and literary uncomformity began in the early 1930s. Arrested in 1934, he was exiled first to Cherdyn' in the Urals and later to Voronezh. Allowed to return to Moscow he was re-arrested there in 1938. His last harrowing years are fully documented by his wife, Nadezhda Yakovlevna, in *Hope against Hope* (1970). He probably died in a transit camp near Vladivostok in December 1938. A decimated edition of his poetry was published in the Soviet Union in 1972.

1.   Возьми на радость из моих ладоней
         Немного солнца и немного мёда
         Как нам велели пчёлы Персефоны.

4. Не отвязать неприкреплённой лодки,
    Не услыхать в меха обутой тени,
    Не превозмочь в дремучей жизни страха.

7. Нам остаются только поцелуи,
    Мохнатые, как маленькие пчёлы,
    Что умирают, взлетев из улья.

10. Они шуршат в прозрачных дебрях ночи,
    Их родина – дремучий лес Тайгета,
    Их пища – время, медуница, мята.

13. Возьми ж на радость мой подарок,
    Невзрачное сухое ожерелье
    Из мёртвых пчёл, мёд превративших в солнце.

                                        (1920)

Take from my palms to bring you happiness
A little sun and a little honey
As Persephone's bees commanded.

One cannot unmoor an unmoored boat,
One cannot hear the fur-shod shadow,
One cannot overcome the fear in life's dense forest.

For us, all that's left are kisses,
Furry, like the little bees,
That die when they leave the hive.

They hum in night's transparent tangled depths,
Their country is the dense forest of Tygetos,
Their food is Time, lungwort and mint.

Do take my present for your happiness,
A dried-up unattractive necklace
Of dead bees that made a sun from honey.

In the terrible flux of life Mandel'shtam sees poetry as the
only consolation. The tone of the poem reflects these mixed
feelings: in the first stanza the creative act is seen as a source of
potential joy and happiness, yet the negated perfective infinitives in the second deny the possibility of rising above the flux
and terrors of life. A feeling of resignation is conveyed by the
только of the third stanza, but even then the bees are still a

source of joy – *поцелуи*. The particle *ж* introduces a tone of positive assertion into the final stanza, thus returning to the feelings of the first stanza. These tonal changes are the key to this difficult but excellent poem. Structurally, it is circular, viz. its initial modest affirmation quickly polarises into a negative resignation, but this polarity reverses into joyful affirmation.

The poem consists of five stanzas, each an independent syntactical unit. Within each stanza each line is a complete sense-unit. Both these features give the poem a certain classic weightiness, a lapidary quality appropriate to both tone and content. Narrowing the focus still further, the poem is composed of five tercets of iambic pentameter with an additional syllable, continually and subtly exploiting metre/rhythm counterpoint and metric irregularity, e.g. *взлетев* in the third stanza is within an anapaestic foot, serving to isolate and emphasise it. Appropriately, for such a 'classical' poem, rhyme is not used.

The world of this poem is one of objects belonging to the natural world: sun, honey, bees, thickets, forests, plants, with the notable exception of two abstractions: fear and Time. Despite its being figurative and intellectually complex this poem expresses itself clearly and visually. Its vocabulary closely reflects this observation: its lapidary quality must to some extent be due to a striking predominance of nouns over verbs and adjectives. However, these 'ordinary' words are combined in a most extraordinary way, e.g. *мохнатые поцелуи; прозрачные дебри; невзрачное сухое ожерелье/из мёртвых пчёл*, all of which considerably enlivens the classical sub-theme of the poet as $\mu\acute{\epsilon}\lambda\iota\sigma\sigma\alpha$ (a bee) – a noun applied in Greek poetry to poets from their culling the beauties of Nature.

The first stanza introduces this apian sub-theme. A further classical echo appears in the reference to Persephone, the emblem of vegetable life and its burgeoning. Its relatively simple vocabulary is heightened by the transference of the whole stanza to the level of metaphor. A certain spareness pervades because of the complete absence of adjectives and adverbs, while syntactically and rhythmically it approximates to everyday speech. An unobtrusive metre controls what is in fact one sentence extending over the three lines. This natural rhythm and language impart a certain confidence to its sunny tone. It is noteworthy that, rather than speak of the creative act as such, Mandel'shtam prefers the indirect but greater power of metaphor. Equally unobtrusive is a subtle sound play, viz. *м/н/п/л/а/о*.

The second stanza presents a striking tonal change from the sunny Hellenism of the preceding to a pessimistic impersonality. Each line has the same verbal texture, viz. negative verb followed by a qualified object. However, the metaphorical density of each line belies its structural obviousness. The intangible flux of life is conveyed by the metaphor of an already unmoored boat which cannot again be unmoored; the inexorability of Death as the inaudible footfall of a fur-shod shadow, a dark, insuperable fear in the midst of the dense forest of life. A counterpoint of metre and rhythm highlights *отвязать; неприкреплённой; услыхать; не превозмочь.* The initial negative particles very categorically emphasise impossibility, while the three nouns in final position are thereby emphasised, especially *страха*. The end-stopping of the lines, each with virtually the same grammatical structure, gives them the timelessness of a Horatian pronouncement. As in the first stanza the sound pattern is used subtly yet effectively, viz. the unstressed vowels and the consonant *н* in the first line; *m/x/y/a* in the second; and the repeated *p* of the third.

However, despite the pessimism of the second stanza, there *is* a source of joy in life, expressed in the image of *поцелуи* in the first line of the third (l.7), albeit limited by *только*. The logic of the imagery at this point becomes very complex. The poetic word, metaphorically transformed into a kiss as a source of joy, is simultaneously a small, hairy bee which, as we know from the poem in toto, has the Orphic power of transmutation; as such the 'apian' word 'dies', i.e. ceases to exist as a mere word, on leaving the 'poet-hive'. This crabbed explanation scarcely does justice to the splendid metaphoric density of this stanza expressed, not in the clumsy abstractions of criticism, but in a simple, concrete vocabulary. This whole process is conveyed in rhythms very different from the two preceding stanzas. Here, as in the other two, there is a single sentence, but it is syntactically and rhythmically broken, thereby emphasising *мохнатые* and *взлетев*, while the complex counterpoint and metrical irregularity of l.9 give special emphasis to the process of death and rebirth.

No ordinary bees these: their habitat, home and food are all unusual. One associates bees with warm sunny days – these

bees belong to darkest night, a night as dense as *дебри*, yet still
прозрачный, an apparently contradictory epithet. The intima-
tion seems to be that such difficult conditions can prove
'transparent' – allowing the poet to 'see through'. Moreover,
their home is not the traditional sunny Mt Hymettos on Attica,
celebrated for its honey, but the dense forests of wild and
remote Mt Tygetos in the South Peloponnese. Even more
unusual is their diet of mint, lungwort and Time. Again,
through metaphor, Mandel'shtam is conveying complex ideas,
viz. the difficult and unusual conditions in which the vital
transformation of words into poetry takes place. Yet again
these ideas are in a remarkably simple, concrete language of
strong images in unusual combinations. This stanza especially
has a particularly static quality, having only one verb. Syntactically this stanza resembles the second in consisting of three
end-stopped self-sufficient lines. The line-breaks after *родина*
and *пища* and the consequent rhythmic counterpoint serve to
emphasise the unusual nature of what follows. This time the
poet employs different sound effects, viz. l.10 – *а/р/ч/ш*; l.11 –
р/д/т; l.12 – *м/и*.

The assertion of the positive value of his present finds its
expression in the unobtrusive particle *ж*. Although this present
is *невзрачное сухое*, it is still an adornment: *ожерелье*. This is a
special artefact, composed of 'dead bees', words which have
perished in their normal usage; these 'apian' words have
achieved something remarkable – they have reversed the normal process by converting honey into sunlight; they have
transformed the natural world in a unique way. All this again is
conveyed by commonplace nouns and adjectives. The rhythmic
simplicity and open vowel *a* contrast with the crabbed sound of
l.14, the content of which is emphasised by rhythm, isolation
and a subtle use of vowels and consonant groups. Similarly, the
caesura in l.15 strikingly emphasises what follows; in this last
hemistich metrical inversion highlights *мёд* and *солнце*.

ЮРИЙ КА́РЛОВИЧ ОЛЕ́ША

(1889–1960)

The son of an impoverished Polish nobleman, Olesha grew up and spent his early life in Odessa. During the Civil War he fought in the Red Army. On demobilisation he moved to Moscow where he worked with Bulgakov (q.v.) and other writers on *Гудо́к*, the newspaper of the Union of Railwaymen, the most advanced and literate section of the Russian working-class at that time, and a bastion of Menshevism. He worked on it for six years as sub-editor, feature-writer and columnist. During this time he became disillusioned with the increasing bureaucratic intolerance of the new Soviet state.

He achieved instant fame in 1928 with the publication of the novel, *За́висть*, later dramatised as *За́говор чу́вств*, a clever and exuberant satire on trends in Soviet life in the twenties, in which an efficient, Soviet sausage-manufacturer is confronted by an anarchic, drunken, irresponsible individualist. The confrontation is dealt with so ingeniously that the novel has been interpreted as both anti- and pro-Soviet. His fear, expressed in this novel, that man is being dehumanised by the cult of the collective appears in his short stories, e.g., *Вишнёвая ко́сточка* (1931) and his play, *Спи́сок благодея́ний* (1931). His literary swan-song was a long, defiant speech at the First Congress of the Union of Soviet Writers in 1934. He was imprisoned in 1938 and again after the War, but was released during the 'Thaw' and allowed to pursue journalism in his last years.

Зависть

(1928)

Я не буду уже ни красивым, ни знаменитым. Я не приду из маленького города в столицу. Я не буду ни полководцем, ни наркомом, ни учёным, ни бегуном, ни авантюристом. Я мечтал всю жизнь о необычайной любви. Скоро я вернусь на старую квартиру, в комнату со страшной кроватью. Там грустное соседство: вдова Прокопович. Ей лет сорок пять, а во дворе её называют 'Анечка'. Она варит обеды для артели парикмахеров. Кухню она устроила в коридоре. В тёмной впадине – плита. Она кормит кошек. Тихие худые кошки взлетают за её руками гальваническими движениями. Она расшвыривает им какие-то потроха. Пол поэтому украшен как бы перламутровыми плевками. Однажды я поскользнулся, наступив на чьё-то сердце – маленькое и туго оформленное, как каштан. Она ходит опутанная кошками и жилами животных. В её руке сверкает нож. Она раздирает кишки локтями, как принцесса паутину.

Вдова Прокопович стара, жирна и рыхла. Её можно выдавливать, как ливерную колбасу. Утром я застигал её у раковины в коридоре. Она была неодета и улыбалась мне *женской* улыбкой. У дверей её, на табуретке, стоял таз, и в нём плавали вычесанные волосы.

Вдова Прокопович – символ моей мужской унижённости. Получается так: Пожалуйста, я готова, ошибитесь ночью дверьми, я нарочно не запру, я приму вас. Будем жить, наслаждаться. А мечты о необычайной любви бросьте. Всё прошло. Вот и сами вы какой стали, сосед: толстенький, в укоротившихся брючках. Ну, что вам ещё нужно? Та? Тонкорукая? Воображаемая? С яйцевидным личиком? Оставьте. Вы папаша уже. Валяйте, а? Кровать у меня замечательная. Покойник на лотерее выиграл. Стёганое одеяло. Присмотрю за вами. Пожалею. А?

Иногда явную неприличность выражал её взгляд. Иногда при встрече со мной из горла её выкатывается некий маленький звук, круглая голосовая капля, вытолкнутая спазмой восторга.

Я не папаша, стряпуха! Я не пара тебе, гадина!

I shall no longer be either handsome or famous. I shall not come to the capital from some small town. I shall not be a military leader, a commissar, a scientist, a runner or adventurer. All my life I've dreamed of an unusual love. Soon I shall return to my old flat, to the room with the awful bed. I have a sad neighbour there: the widow Prokopovich. She's about forty-five, and known locally as 'Anechka'. She cooks for a hairdressers' collective. She's set up her kitchen in the corridor. There's a stove in a dark cavity. She feeds cats. Quiet, skinny cats fly up to her hands with galvanic movements. She slings them innards of some sort, so the floor is adorned as it were by mother-of-pearl gobbets of spit. Once I slipped by treading on something's heart – it was small and neatly formed like a chestnut. She walks around entangled in cats and animals' veins. A knife flashes in her hand. She tears the guts up with her elbows spread wide, like a princess among cobwebs.

The widow Prokopovich is old, fat and flabby. You could squeeze her out like a liver-sausage. In the morning I'd catch her at the wash-basin in the corridor. She was not dressed and would smile at me with a *womanly* smile. On a stool by her door was a basin with combed-out hair floating in it.

The widow Prokopovich is a symbol of my masculine degradation. It turns out like this: please, I'm ready, come in the wrong door at night, I'll leave it unlocked on purpose. I'll take you. Let's live together and enjoy ourselves. As for your dreams of an unusual love, give them up. That's all over. Look what's become of you, neighbour: paunchy, with your trousers too short. Well, what else do you want? Her? The one with the delicate hands? The imaginary one? The one with an egg-shaped face? Give her up. You're old enough to be her father. Come on, how about it? I've got a remarkable bed. My late husband won it in the lottery. It's got a quilt. I'll look after you. I'll feel sorry for you. How about it, eh?

Her expression sometimes shows obvious indecency. Sometimes when she meets me a little sound rolls out of her throat, a pure drop of sound squeezed out by a spasm of delight.

Cook, I'm not old enough to be her father! I'm not the one for you, you repulsive object!

In this dramatic monologue the first-person narrator, the anti-hero of the book, bemoans his fate and what he considers are the intentions of the widow Prokopovich towards him. He bemoans in a mixture of resigned self-pity for himself and aggressive revulsion towards the widow. Self-pity is evoked at the beginning by the repetition of the first person singular pronoun with a series of negated verbs in the future tense and the incremental negation of the repeated *ни*. The details of his flat are intended to evoke feelings of pity. Further on it is evoked by the contrast of the repellent details in the main body of the passage with the poignant *Я мечтал всю жизнь о необычайной любви.* His revulsion is expressed in his choice of adjectives: *стара, жирна и рыхла*; in his choice of verbs: *её можно выдавливать*; and the manner in which he depicts her activities: *она расшвыривает им какие-то потроха; она ходит опутанная кошками и жилами животных.*

The passage is structured from the general to the particular: the first four sentences generalise his condition, the last one serving as a springboard for a grotesquely detailed illustration of his dismal love-life, climaxing in his unspoken rebellion against her possibly imaginary advances. The passage achieves unity by its consistent tone and linguistic expression of revulsion.

Strong images of degradation and repulsion permeate the passage: *старую квартиру; страшной кроватью; в тёмной впадине – плита; пол поэтому украшен как бы перламутровыми плевками; она раздирает кишки локтями; в нём плавали вычесанные волосы; стряпуха!; гадина!.* To convey this the largely simple and concrete, noun-dominated vocabulary emphasises sense-impressions, especially the visual. Much of the passage's impact comes from its phraseology which consistently and strikingly emphasises the narrator's perceptions of his repulsive and degraded situation, e.g. *перламутровыми плевками; чьё-то сердце; опутанная кошками и жилами животных; ?енской улыбкой; в укоротившихся брючках.*

The narrative viewpoint of the speaking-voice of this passage is announced immediately – *я*; this viewpoint has to be remembered in assessing the truth and significance of the degrading and repulsive details presented. In a series of staccato, paratactic, initially-stressed sentences the narrator announces his unequivocal future failure, emphasised by the heavily incremental repetition of negative particles and clausal anaphora. It should be noted that the things he will not achieve all belong to an immature, romantic conception of the world. A subtle change of tense, from the future to the equivalent of a perfect continuous, directs our attention to another of his romantic fantasies – *необычайной любви*, and serves as an introduction to a grotesquely detailed account of the degraded state of his hopes. Completely avoiding sentence co-ordination, the series of paratactic clauses in this paragraph faithfully reproduces the spare but controlled rhythms of an educated, narrative speaking-voice. The shocking contrast appears between the muted sentence rhythms and their content – Gogol'`'`s 'tidal waves' of grotesque detail are quite absent here.

The narrator's self-pity continues to be apparent in the two parallel prepositional phrases (which also serve to narrow the focus) following *я скоро вернусь* – in each note the significant adjectives *старую* and *страшную*. Moreover, this is extended by the adjective *грустное* beyond his dwelling to a female neighbour, significantly referred to as *вдова*. Her age and activities are presented in an unusually neutral manner, with the exception of the unthinkable implications of the stove's situation *в тёмной впадине*. Surprise is achieved by a sudden digression, supremely effective in its brevity – *она кормит кошек*. At this point the narrator employs his considerable linguistic resources to convey his revulsion at feeding-time. This is achieved by a now subtle, now striking use of diction. The cats are seen not only to *взлетать* but also to fly up in a surprising manner: *гальваническими движениями*. Moreover, she acts with panache: *расшвыривает*, and what she throws about are namelessly horrible: *какие-то потроха*. The results of her actions are conveyed visually by bathos and a horrifically effective metaphor: *пол поэтому украшен* is linked with the alliterative *как бы перламутровыми плевками*. Slipping on one such object (N.B. the effectiveness of the deliberately indefinite *чьё-то*), he studies it with a mixture of repulsion and fascination, forcing us also to imagine it through the vivid simile *как каштан*. Surprise is used again to effect in the grotesquely exaggerated image, a bizarre echo of Byron's 'She walks in beauty ...': *Она ходит опутанная кошками и жилами животных*, heightened by a complex system of assonance and alliteration. Amid the gloom and mess of cats and offal flashes a knife. The final image of her activities is very striking in the use of an upward comparison, the Sleeping Beauty simile, to refer to the tenor of her tearing animal guts apart with her elbows spread wide. (N.B. guttural and labial alliteration.)

Maintaining the same rhythms of a narrative speaking-voice, the narrator switches to the physical appearance of the widow. He immediately emphasises her unattractive appearance with three adjectives in the short form, thereby somewhat heightening these qualities. As if it were not enough to call her *жирна и рыхла*, he has recourse to the repellent simile of squeezing out a liver-sausage. From general he moves to particular observations of her at her toilet – not the best time to see anyone! His fear of her advances almost attains paranoia in the emphatic *женской*, but he deliberately evokes disgust with the heavily alliterated and vivid *в нём плавали вычесанные волосы.*

In the next paragraph he ostensibly reports a different viewpoint, and in so doing provides a far less romantic image of himself than what is implied in the offended machismo of *вдова Прокопович – символ моей мужской унижённости.* A change of sentence rhythm is immediately apparent in this section, reproducing the clipped, telegraphic rhythms of semi-articulate, elliptical speech. The diction and phraseology of the intellectual are absent here. The whole section from *А мечты* ... to *Вы папаша уже* rapidly destroys his castles in the air in its choice of diction: *толстенький, в укоротившихся брючках* (N.B. the diminutive), and syntax, e.g. the harsh, but perceptive brevity of *Та? Тонкорукая? Воображаемая? С яйцевидным личиком?.* Moreover, she does not hesitate to appeal to his lowest instincts by changing the subject from his romantic fantasy to the primeval realities of her bedroom.

The final paragraph expresses his offended pride at her suggestions; he even sees obscenity in the way she looks at him, and excels in his interpretation of a sound she makes with a splendidly evocative use of diction: the *круглая голосовая капля, вытолкнутая* by a spasm of delight is not simply emitted but *выкатывается.* The passage ends in a paralleled splutter of rage and offended dignity.

ВЛАДИ́МИР ВЛАДИ́МИРОВИЧ МАЯКО́ВСКИЙ

(1893–1930)

One of the leading figures of Russian Futurism, Mayakovsky is also a major figure in twentieth-century poetry, ranking alongside Eliot, Valéry and Rilke in his impact on the content and form of modern poetry. In the years of the First World War he achieved notoriety for his personal flamboyance, his 'slaps in the face for public taste' and his remarkable poetry, which by 1913 already had the features of his mature style. He accepted the October Revolution unhesitatingly, devising propaganda posters, slogans and rhymes, and giving public recitations. Beneath a loud exterior was a complex, confused personality, reflected in his more lyrical verse. A variety of reasons is adduced for his suicide in 1930, varying between tertiary syphilis and discontent with the political situation in the U.S.S.R.

His verse is intentionally revolutionary both in form and content to accord with the new revolutionary society. Rejecting the traditions of both Symbolism and of the nineteenth-century classics (which he wanted to 'throw overboard'), he juxtaposed words and images in new and shocking ways – a juxtaposition reinforced by masterly sound-effects: unusual assonances, rhymes and rhythms. A notable feature is that many of his poems were printed *с разбивкой* (in steps) for visual and declamatory purposes. He aggressively avoided standard vocabulary and imagery, sometimes to an obscure and absurd degree. All these features can be found in his major long poems, especially *Облако в штанах* (1915), *Флейта-позвоночник* (1915), *Влади́мир Ильи́ч Ле́нин* (1924) and *Во весь го́лос* (1930). A well-known direct poetic descendant, especially in terms of colloquial diction, imagery and layout, is Yevtushenko (q.v.).

Наш Марш
(1917)

1. Бейте в площади бунтов топот!
    Выше, гордых голов гряда!
    Мы разливом второго потопа
    Перемоем миров города.

5. Дней бык пег.
    Медленна лет арба.
    Наш бог бег.
    Сердце наш барабан.

9. Есть ли наших золот небесней?
    Нас ли сжалит пули оса?
    Наше оружие – наши песни.
    Наше золото – звенящие голоса.

13. Зеленью ляг, луг,
    Выстели дно дням.
    Радуга, дай дуг
    Лет быстролётным коням.

17. Видите, скушно звёзд небу!
    Без него наши песни вьём.
    Эй, Большая Медведица! требуй,
    Чтоб на небо взяли живьём.

21. Радости пей! Пой!
    В жилах весна разлита.
    Сердце, бей бой!
    Грудь наша – медь литавр.

Beat out the tramp of revolt in the square!
Up, row of proud heads!
With the waters of a second Deluge
We'll wash every city in the world.

The ox of days is pied.
The cart of years is slow.
Our god is speed.
The heart is our drum.

Is there a gold more heavenly than ours?
Shall we feel the bullet's wasp-sting?
Our weapons are our songs.
Our gold is our ringing voices.

Meadow, spread out a green carpet
And make a floor for the days!
Rainbow, make a shaft-bow
For the swift steeds of the years.

See, the starry sky is bored.
We can make up songs without it.
Hey, Great Bear, demand
That we're taken up alive into the heavens!

Drink joys! Sing them!
Spring runs in our veins.
Heart, beat out battle!
Our breast is a brazen kettledrum.

This short, frequently anthologised poem illustrates all the
features typical of Mayakovsky's poetry. Its theme is the
unique and remarkable nature of the 'march' or coming of the
revolutionary army. In writing what is fundamentally a
declamatory poem Mayakovsky has adopted an aggressive,
excited, hyperbolic tone and a language entirely adequate to it.

He has not adopted a logically developing structure, but
rather a series of loosely-linked hyperbolic claims. The poem
may possibly be divided after the third stanza, viz. stanzas 1–3
might loosely be called 'descriptive', whereas stanzas 4–6 present a peculiar kind of apotheosis. The poem's claims are
presented in six stanzas, alternating in rhythmic structure and
versification. Stanzas 1, 3 and 5 consist of four end-stopped
lines (except ll.3 and 4) with four accentual stresses, rhyming
abab (*a* – truncated, *b* – masculine); stanzas 2, 4 and 6 of four
end-stopped lines with three accentual stresses, rhyming *abab*
(*a* – masculine, *b* – truncated, i.e. the reverse of 1, 3, 5). This
complex, skilful structure is the framework for an almost
outrageous use of diction and imagery, conveyed by a simple,
concrete, but highly emotive vocabulary, appealing to the
visual and aural.

In general terms, his considerable use of imperatives reflects the declamatory nature of the poem. His boldness appears in the dynamic linking of a quite simple vocabulary, e.g. *бык дней; оса пули; арба лет*, and revolutionary collectivity is emphasised by the frequent use of the first person plural.

The first line (like many others) begins with an imperative whose initial consonant is echoed in *б* and *n* in the rest of the line. This aggressive, stirring introductory line is heightened by a number of phonic effects: *Бейте в площади бунтов топот*, i.e. the repetition of the consonants *б/n/в* (devoiced) and *m*, and the vowel *o*. Furthermore, the essentially trochaic beat emphasises the martial tone.

This is succeeded by another command, in elliptical form. The line-break after *выше* emphasises both it and the striking alliteration of the guttural *г*. Were it not for the nature of the theme and tone, such effects, within only two lines, would seem excessive. Unexpectedly, but highly appropriately, the next two lines (3 and 4) are made up of one sweeping sentence with effective positional emphasis on the (significantly *future* perfective) verb, *перемоем*, the moral cleansing of the world's cities by this essentially urban revolution. In its usage here the prefix *пере-* extends the action to all the objects in question. The irresistible sweep of the revolutionary flood finds its phonic equivalence in the alliteration of the vowels *u* and *o*.

The second stanza pulls the reader up short in many ways. The rhythm suddenly changes, and the rhythmic and metric stress coincide almost like drum-beats. The striking metaphor of l.5 is reinforced by consonantal and vocalic cacophony. That the slow passage of time should be likened to an ox is clear and effective, but its piebald nature may simply be a convenient rhyme. This image extends to the *арба лет* to which it is presumably yoked, emphasised by the weighty *медленна* amidst all the monosyllables. Speed finds a very appropriate phonetic equivalence in the alliterative consonants and short vowels of l.7, viz. *наш бог бег*. The martial spirit of the new army is heard in the rapping of *барабан*.

Reverting to the rhythmic and metrical structure of stanza 1, stanza 3 emphasises the absence of the usual military trappings of guns and gold, heightened by the alliteration of the sibilants *ж/ш/с/з*. The unusual *золот* of l.9 (in the genitive plural) points out that this is a property of every revolutionary soldier;

moreover, *небесное* is its nature, the vowels and sibilants of *есть* and *небесней* echoing each other. The invincibility of the revolutionary army is emphasised by the striking metaphor, *оса пули*, and phonetic elements, viz. the use of the consonants *с/ж/л* and the vowels *а* and *и*. The novelty of song and poetry being the weapons of the revolutionary army is rendered by the two boldly end-stopped lines 11 and 12, while putting contrastive emphasis on *оружие – песни, золота – голоса* by very effective parallelism.

The apostrophic fourth stanza is as striking as the second, albeit subtly different. Natural phenomena are called upon to co-operate, emphasised by the arresting dactylic and spondaic rhythm of ll.13, 14 and 15. Still more emphasis is added by the alliteration of *л, д* and *г* and a subtle use of varied vowel sounds: *е-я-у* in succession in l.13, *ы-и-о-я* in l.14, *а-у-ай-у* in l.15. The striking polysyllabic epithet of l.16 is emphasised by its phonic contrasts with *лет* and *коням* viz. *ле-/-лё-, -ым/-ям*.

The fifth stanza asserts that the revolutionary army does not need starry nights to make its songs, a typical piece of Mayakovskian iconoclasm, so it could replace the useless stars as a new constellation. Another feature typical of Mayakovsky is his personification of inanimate objects, in this case the night sky. Its broken, conversational rhythm and harsh vowel music are discreetly held together by a regular but unobtrusive metric structure and rhyme scheme. This stanza is unusual in being virtually devoid of the wide variety of devices employed in the previous four stanzas, although attention should be drawn to the sibilants of ll.17 and 18 and the plosives of ll.19 and 20.

However, the musical element is picked up again in the last stanza, yet again subtly different from stanzas 2 and 4. The enthusiasm of l.21 is heightened by the alliterative *n* and the diapason of vowels *а/о/у/ей/ой*. The vigour of the new revolutionary army is conveyed by a wild synaesthesia, which succeeds in the context of a poem full of all kinds of bold poetic devices. The excitement of l.21 is carried into the rhyme of l.23, where alliteration emphasises the beating of the martial heart. In the final line the percussion metaphor has its own subtle music in *-удь/-едь* and *наша ... литавр*.

ИСААК ЭММАНУЙЛОВИУ БÁБЕЛЬ

(1894–1941)

Born in Odessa, the only son of a highly ambitious and successful business representative, Babel' had a secure, if confined, semi-assimilated Jewish upbringing: he was expected to learn Hebrew, struggle at Stolyarski's 'violin factory', attend heder and follow a standard education at the Nicholas I Commercial School, which he entered in 1905. At the latter institution he met the real Odessa and French literature, which ultimately led him to reject Jewish culture in favour of Russian.

He was sent by his father to the Institute of Business Studies in Kiev in 1911, where he befriended the highly cultured Gronfein family, whose youngest daughter, Yevgeniya, he was later to marry. Upon graduation at the end of 1915 he moved illegally to Petrograd and while there had two stories published in Gor'ky's *Хрóника*, around which the Futurist set gathered. He enlisted in the army in October 1917, but was back in Petrograd by March 1918, working for the Cheka and in the '*продотряды*'. After his marriage in 1919 and return south, he was assigned by the Odessa Communist Party Committee in summer 1920 as a war-correspondent in Budyonny's First Cavalry.

Despite poor health he spent the early twenties writing and had four stories published in 1924 in *LEF*, causing a minor literary sensation and Budyonny's undying enmity. Despite considerable emotional problems, continuing poor health and shortage of money, Babel' continued to write stories and plays well into the early thirties. He spoke at the First Congress of the Union of Soviet Writers in 1934 and, despite the death of his patron, Gor'ky, in 1936, still lived relatively well until his sudden arrest in 1939, officially dying in a labour-camp in March 1941.

His small output belongs largely to the twenties, his fame

resting on *Конáрмия* (1926), impressions of his service with Budyonny's Cossacks in Poland, which gain their power and strength from being a non-violent intellectual's repelled, determined and fascinated effort to convey, in a uniquely visual style, fearsome brutality, violence and terror. His *Расскáзы* and *Одéсские расскáзы*, mainly written in the twenties, are accounts of various aspects of Jewish life in Odessa, including his own childhood and the underworld. His two plays, *Закáт* (1928) and *Марúя* (1935), are interesting, though not memorable attempts to convey the decline of the old pre-Revolutionary order.

Переход через Збруч

(1926)

Начдив шесть донёс о том, что Новоград-Волынск взят сегодня на рассвете. Штаб выступил из Крапивно, и наш обоз шумливым арьергардом растянулся по шоссе, идущему от Бреста до Варшавы и построенному на мужичьих костях Николаем Первым.

Поля пурпурного мака цветут вокруг нас, полуденный ветер играет в желтеющей ржи, девственная гречиха встаёт на горизонте, как стена дальнего монастыря. Тихая Волынь изгибается, Волынь уходит от нас в жемчужный туман берёзовых рощ, она вползает в цветистые пригорки и ослабевшими руками путается в зарослях хмеля. Оранжевое солнце катится по небу, как отрубленная голова, нежный свет загорается в ущельях туч, штандарты заката веют над нашими головами. Запах вчерашней крови и убитых лошадей каплет в вечернюю прохладу. Почерневший Збруч шумит и закручивает пенистые узлы своих порогов. Мосты разрушены, и мы переезжаем реку вброд. Величавая луна лежит на волнах. Лошади по спину уходят в воду, звучные потоки сочатся между сотнями лошадиных ног. Кто-то тонет и звонко порочит Богородицу. Река усеяна чёрными квадратами телег, она полна гула, свиста и песен, гремящих поверх лунных змей и сияющих ям.

Divisional Commander 6 reported that Novograd-Volynsk had fallen at dawn today. Headquarters moved out of Krapivno and our transport, noisily bringing up the rear, was stretched out along the highway extending from Brest to Warsaw and built on peasants' bones by Nicholas I.

Fields of purple poppies are in bloom all around us, the noonday wind plays in the yellow rye and on the horizon the virginal buckwheat looks like the walls of a distant monastery. The quiet Volyn' winds by, disappearing into a pearly haze of birch woods, crawls into flower-covered hillocks and gets its feeble arms tangled up in hop thickets. The orange sun rolls down the sky like a severed head, its soft light blazes in cloud canyons, and sunset's standards flutter above our heads. The smell of yesterday's blood and dead horses drips into the cool evening air. The dark, noisy Zbrucz ties up the foamy knots of its rapids. The bridges are down, so we ford the river. A magnificent moon lies on the waves. Horses go up to their backs in the water, and sonorous streams trickle between hundreds of horses' legs. Somebody goes under, loudly cursing the Virgin. The river is covered with the black squares of carts, and is full of rumbling, whistling and songs ringing out above moon-snakes and shining pits.

In the detached, remote voice of a military dispatch this extract provides a brief, impressionistic description of the crossing of the river Zbrucz (formerly marking the Ukrainian–Polish border) at sunset. This military remoteness is apparent in the first line – *начдив шесть донёс*, and the narrator's deliberate detachment from events, despite his presence there (N.B. the subtle shifts, as if from first person to third person narration), is conveyed through a predominantly visual imagery – all is seen through the cold, though uniquely sensitive, camera-eye of a deliberately aloof observer. Syntax contributes greatly in the tension between the striking expressionist imagery in which the narrator's observations are recorded and a diaristic, rather abrupt parataxis and rhythm of S/V/O clauses (the only conjunction used is *u* and that sparingly). Similarly, a tension exists between the present-tense observations (or snap-shots) recorded in the passage and its disarmingly simple structure, viz. the first paragraph provides a brief location, while the second is a report en route. Although between individual sentences there are some astonishingly abrupt changes of focus, the passage is saved from dissolution by the narrator's discernible and guiding presence providing an overall unity and direction.

The predominantly visual imagery of this ostensibly naturalistic passage is conveyed in relatively simple and concrete vocabulary, dominated by nouns and adjectives (N.B. the high frequency of participles and virtual absence of adverbs), but what is most memorable is its striking and idiosyncratic phraseology, especially in its sometimes futuristic similes and metaphors, e.g. *жемчужный туман берёзовых рощ; как отрубленная голова; штандарты заката; запах вчерашней крови и убитых лошадей каплет; лунных змей и сияющих ям.*

The very first sentence announces a Soviet military situation in its use of the stump-compound *начдив*, the verb *донёс*, and the participle *взят*. The first paragraph contains the rhythmic structures which are more or less maintained throughout the whole extract, viz. the most basic word-order of subject/verb/non-verbal predicate, and parataxis or the use of the simple conjunction *и*. At the same time the third sentence, in its participially extended predicate, is echoed later in the passage. Moreover, the parallelism of the two participles exhibits another stylistic element: the shocking contrast between the neutral *идущему от Бреста до Варшавы* and *построенному на мужичьих костях Николаем Первым*, although this is a typical cliché of the period.

The second, major paragraph maintains the passage's typical rhythm but, unlike the first paragraph, comprises a series of vivid visual images with expressive blocks of colour, emphasised by the unexpected simile *как стена дальнего монастыря*. The use of the present tense and *вокруг нас* increase the sense of the immediacy of a report. The next group of paratactic clauses concerns the Volyn' which is virtually personified by a wide variety of verbs; *изгибается; уходит; вползает; путается*. Whereas Babel' appears to avoid the adverb, using instead, as in the first paragraph, an effective metaphorical phrase, adjectives and nouns command particular attention. From this scene there is a sudden shift into areas of colour in the sky, depicting the process of sunset. This shift effects a very strong contrast because the setting sun is described thus: *катится по небу*, emphasised by the deliberately shocking and improbable Futuristic simile – *как отрубленная голова*. The next clause suddenly dims from orange to a *нежный свет,* depicted as burning *в ущельях туч*, a more acceptable visual metaphor. Appropriately, a military, almost eighteenth-century metaphor is employed – *штандарты заката* – to convey the fading light of sunset. The overall effect is one of deliberate and violent contrast.

Although this extract is one of the observing eye, the next, completely isolated clause suddenly assails the sense of smell and, as earlier, phrases are used in parallel to achieve the maximum effect: *вчерашней крови и убитых лошадей*. This clause is made all the more memorable by the strange synaesthesia of *запах ... каплет*. These repellent details of war contrast strongly with the implied calm of Nature in the phrase, *в вечернюю прохладу*. With a by now accustomed rapidity it is dark and the rearguard has reached the Zbrucz, a very different river from the Volyn′; all this is conveyed by *Почерневший Збруч шумит*. As with the Volyn′ Babel′ chooses to personify in striking imagery the presence on the Zbrucz of rapids: *закручивает пенистые узлы своих порогов*, employing alliteration – *п/р/с/ш/ч/у* – to echo their sound.

From being a detached observer the narrator reminds us of his presence in the bald and almost off-hand simplicity of *Мосты разрушены, и мы переезжаем реку вброд*. After this his attention returns to the confused scene of the fording of the river. Again appears the contrast between Man and Nature. The scene is now described thus: *Величавая луна лежит на волнах* (an isolated sentence expressively alliterated with *в/л/а*), in which attention is directed first to the horses in two paratactic clauses where sound and sight are cleverly blended in the splendidly musical *звучные потоки сочатся между сотнями лошадиных ног*. This is linked by sound to *звонко* in the casual but resonant *кто-то тонет и звонко порочит Богородицу*. The final scene is both visually memorable in the contrasts between *чёрными квадратами телег* and the *лунных змей и сияющих ям*, and rhythmically striking in its use of contrast between *река усеяна чёрными квадратами телег* and *она полна гула, свиста и песен, гремящих поверх лунных змей и сияющих ям*, where a cumulative and also contrasting effect is achieved by three unqualified nouns (denoting sounds) being followed by the very different sounds and rhythms of the visual *гремящих поверх лунных змей и сияющих ям*.

СЕРГЕ́Й АЛЕКСА́НДРОВИЧ ЕСЕ́НИН

(1895–1925)

Born in the village of Konstantinovo, near Ryazan', Yesenin was brought up in the heart of rural Old Russia by his peasant grandfather, a member of an Old Believer sect. He wrote verse from childhood on and made a precocious, colourful entrance, dressed in a peasant smock and reciting his apparently artless bucolic-religious poetry, into the pre-Revolutionary literary salons of Petersburg and Moscow, where he was welcomed as an unlettered genius.

He greeted the October Revolution enthusiastically, writing a number of unmemorable, Utopian poems about it. At the same time he was a member of the 'Imaginist' group of poets, a Soviet counterpart of Anglo-American Imagism.

In his pre-Revolutionary poetry, posing half-consciously as the spontaneous voice of Holy Russia, Yesenin lamented with gentle melancholy the passing of an idealised countryside, invaded by the modern age, but in the twenties he was torn by nostalgia for a lost Old Russia, and the lure of the city with its taverns and prostitutes. This quandary was expressed in his two long poems, *Русь сове́тская* and *Русь уходя́щая* (both 1924).

He sought escape through travel in Europe and America and a legendary debauchery, having married the American dancer, Isadora Duncan, in 1922. Disillusioned after Isadora's macabre death, he returned to the U.S.S.R. in 1923, only to re-marry and travel somewhat more quietly around Persia. By now a hopeless alcoholic, continually in trouble for acts of 'hooliganism', he hanged himself in 1925 in a Leningrad hotel, after writing a farewell poem in his own blood. Despite long official disapproval Yesenin has always ranked in popularity alongside Pushkin and Mayakovsky among ordinary Russian readers.

111

Сорокоуст

(1920)

Видели ли вы,
Как бежит по степям,
В туманах озёрных кроясь,
Железной ноздрёй храпя
5.　На лапах чугунных поезд?
А за ним
По большой траве,
Как на празднике отчаянных гонок,
Тонкие ноги закидывая к голове,
10.　Скачет красногривый жеребёнок?

Милый, милый, смешной дуралей,
Ну куда он, куда он гонится?
Неужель он не знает, что живых коней
Победила стальная конница?
15.　Неужель он не знает, что в полях бессиянных
Той поры не вернёт его бег,
Когда пару красивых степных россиянок
Отдавал за коня печенег?
По-иному судьба на торгах перекрасила
20.　Наш разбуженный скрежетом плёс,
И за тысячи пудов конской кожи и мяса
Покупают теперь паровоз.

Have you seen the train on its cast-iron feet
Rushing through the steppes,
Hiding in the mists of the lakes,
Snorting through its iron nostril?
And close behind,
As though in a desperate race at a gymkhana,
A red-maned colt is galloping
Through the tall grass,
Flinging its slender legs
As high as its head.

The dear, dear comic little fool,
Where, where is he racing to?
Surely he knows that living horses
Have been vanquished by the steel cavalry?

Surely he knows that his gallop in the gloomy plain
Will not bring back the days
When the Pecheneg would give back
A couple of beautiful Russian girls from the steppes
In exchange for a steed?
At the auctions fate has altered
Our still, broad waters,
Awakened by the grinding of trains,
And for tons and tons
Of horse-flesh and skin
One now buys a locomotive.

On seeing a foal trying to race a steam locomotive across the steppes, the author meditates on the fate of the horse in modern Russia, on the supersession of the living horse by the 'iron' horse. The tone of the poem changes according to his reactions to the subject-matter. His affection for the foal is signalled by his addressing it as *милый, милый, смешной дуралей*; and his sadness at the passing of the horse is conveyed by two rhetorical questions in the second stanza, from *неужель* ... to ... *печенег*. This changes at the end of the poem to anger and horror at the horse's probable fate, from *по-иному* ... to *паровоз*.

The poem could be said to be structured in two ways. In one respect, an observation of a particular horse leads the poet to a general meditation on the fate of the horse in the twentieth century. In another, images of two kinds of 'horse' are juxtaposed, the living and the 'iron' horse, with the implied transformation of the former into a means for obtaining the latter. These ideas are presented in the form of five rhetorical questions and a brutal, final answer. This overall structure contains another structure – that of each stanza, viz. the first presents a simple unrhetorical contrast between the two types of 'horse', whereas the second builds up through a series of melancholy questions to a horrible climax.

Although the poem's ideas are arranged in this relatively simple manner, its formal structure is highly complex and irregular, as though reflecting the poet's changing feelings, i.e. strict regularity would not be appropriate to his melancholy and anger. Not only does each stanza differ in length (10 and 12 lines respectively), but so do the lines themselves: in the first stanza they extend to form two long sentences; in the second they form two couplets and two four-line sentences. Metrically the poem exhibits the same irregularity – the first stanza varies between one and four accents per line, whereas the second alternates between four and three. The feminine and truncated rhymes of the first stanza encapsulate the two sentences with the schema *abcbc* and *defef*, while the masculine, dactylic and truncated ones of the second form three quatrains – *ababcdcdefef*.

The imagery, quite appropriately, consists of a series of equine images, an interweaving of flesh and steel, conveyed in a simple, concrete, predominantly visual language. This is true despite the fact that much of it is used to illustrate a 'dead' metaphor, i.e. the 'iron' horse. Indeed, the concrete, direct nature of Yesenin's vision is well exemplified by this poem, since it contains only one abstract noun – *судьба*. He uses verbs in the first part to emphasise movement, shifting to a wider framework in the second. Although he has little recourse to adverbs, he employs a wide and significant variety of adjectives, notably three describing metal, viz. *железный; чугунный; стальной*. Unlike his contemporary, Mayakovsky, in this poem Yesenin limits the use of unusual phraseology. However, what he does use is in keeping with his strong visual sense, i.e. *железной ноздрёй храпя; на лапах чугунных поезд; разбуженный скрежетом плёс* and the almost callous *судьба на торгах*.

Yesenin achieves a sense of immediacy in the first line with *видели ли вы* which he maintains right up to the final ghastly image. The picture of the 'iron' horse is built up by a succession of striking images – *в туманах озёрных кроясь; железной ноздрёй храпя; на лапах чугунных*. The movement and power of the steam-locomotive is aptly conveyed by the rhythmic surge of the five-line sentence, culminating in the most important word – *поезд*. The first half of the first stanza is closely paralleled in structure, imagery and rhythm by the second – *жеребёнок* is the last word, as is *поезд*; there are many short, unstressed vowels, effectively conveying the dominant racing image – a certain doomed futility seems inherent in *отчаянных*. The second half is given greater rhythmic effect by the subtly alliterative use of *к* and *г*. Both parts are clinched, yet separated, by the rhyme scheme.

The tone of the initial part of the second stanza is very

kilfully conveyed, each word carefully chosen, especially *милый, милый, смешной дуралей/ну куда он, куда он* – insistent epetition combined with the long vowels and diphthongs. Furthermore, the line-break after *ну куда он* aptly emphasises he futility of this literal and historic race, as does *неужель он е знает* in the third line. There is a powerful finality in the solation of *победила стальная конница* – the last word emphaised by its rhyming with *гонится*. Pity, sadness and melancholy are augmented still more by the repetition in l.15 of *неужель он не знает*, especially since the foal obviously cannot know of the implied inexorable march of technology. However, a brief vision of former glories is given in the second quatrain, heightened by an apt use of archaisms – *бессиянных; россиянок; коня; печенег*. The anapaestic gallop of these lines suitably culminates with the rhyme-word – *печенег*.

In the last quatrain an abstract, hostile force is at work, which Yesenin emphasises with ugly imagery and sound – *судьба на торгах перекрасила/наш разбуженный скрежетом лёс*. The final horror is conveyed by the isolation of the line *и за тысячи пудов конской кожи и мяса* – so much slaughter to buy a single locomotive, the very last word, clinched by a half-rhyme. The grim imagery of the last two lines is reinforced by the alliterative use of *п/к/с*.

As a whole this poem poignantly and skilfully expresses Yesenin's nostalgia for the passing of rural Old Russia.

МИХАЙЛ АЛЕКСА́НДРОВИЧ ШО́ЛОХОВ

(1905–)

Born into a middle-peasant family in the village of Kruzhilin
then part of the Don Cossack Military Region, now the
Kamensk region of the R.S.F.S.R., Sholokhov himself was no
of Cossack stock, but Russo-Ukrainian. He moved to nearby
Karginsk when he was five, entering the local primary school in
1912. In 1914 he entered a Moscow boarding-school, but
changed school almost as many times as his father changed his
job, finally returning to the Don in 1917, and settling for good
in Karginsk in 1920.

Sholokhov began working at this time, doing a wide variety
of jobs until he decided to join a workers' education course in
Moscow in 1922. In 1925 he succeeded in having published
Донские рассказы and *Лазоревая степь* in 1926 which already
showed his colourful language and strong feelings for the
natural world of South Russia. At the same time he returned to
the Don region where he has stayed ever since. By 1930 he
had completed two parts of his magnum opus, *Тихий Дон*, and
a third part by 1932. Meanwhile he was involved in and
troubled by collectivisation. His experiences of this and Party
dictates turned his attention to writing the first part of
Поднятая целина. He finally finished *Тихий Дон* in 1940. This
enormous and powerful novel is the 'War and Peace' of the
Don Cossacks, showing the tragic inevitability of the break-up
of their traditional way of life. Its objectivity and broad human
sympathy are not at all consistent with Sholokhov's Stalinist
views or the woodenness of *Поднятая целина*, and since the
thirties it has been widely suspected that he pirated the manuscript of the White Cossack writer F. D. Kryukov, who had
died in 1920.

While working as a war-correspondent he began the still
unfinished *Они сражались за родину*. After the War he

resumed work in the Supreme Soviet, to which he had been elected in 1939. In 1954 he was elected to the Secretariat of the Union of Soviet Writers, and was awarded the Order of Lenin in 1955. In 1956 his war-novella, *Судьба́ челове́ка*, was serialised in *Пра́вда*, and the second part of *По́днятая целина́* was published in 1960. Despite considerable objections from the West he was awarded the Nobel Prize in 1965 and, unlike Pasternak, allowed to collect it. He has consistently and strongly attacked the Dissident movement of the late sixties, although he has effectively left the literary scene himself.

Тихий Дон

(1926–40)

Время заплетало дни, как ветер конскую гриву. Перед рождеством внезапно наступила оттепель; сутки шёл дождь, с обдонской горы по ерикам шалая неслась вода; на обнажившихся от снега мысах зазеленели прошлогодняя травка и мшистые плитняки мела; на Дону заедями пенились окраинцы, лёд, трупно синея, вздувался. Невыразимо сладкий запах излучал оголённый чернозём. По Гетманскому шляху, по прошлогодним колеям пузырилась вода. Свежими обвалами зияли глинистые за хутором яры. Южный ветер нёс с Чира томлёные запахи травяного тлена, и в полдни на горизонте уже маячили, как весной, голубые, нежнейшие тени. По хутору около бугров высыпанной у плетней золы стояли рябые лужины. На гумнах оттаивала у скирдов земля, колола в нос прохожего приторная сладость подопревшей соломы. Днями по карнизам куреней с соломенных сосульчатых крыш стекала дегтярная вода, надрывно чечекали на плетнях сороки, и, обуреваемый преждевременным томлением весны, ревел зимовавший на базу у Мирона Григорьевича общественный бугай. Он раскидывал рогами плетни, тёрся о дубовую, изъеденную червоточиной соху, мотал шелковистым подгрудком, копытил на базу рыхлый, напитанный талой водой снег.

На второй день рождества взломало Дон. С мощным хрустом и скрежетом шёл посредине стор. На берег, как сонные чудовищные рыбы, вылезали льдины. За Доном, понукаемые южным волнующим ветром, стремились в неподвижном зыбком беге тополя.

Time had tangled the days as the wind a horse's mane. Just before Christmas a thaw suddenly set in; it rained day and night, raging water rushed down from the Don hills along the dry courses, last year's grass and mossy patches of chalk showed green on the snow-free headlands, the edges of the Don foamed, and the ice turned a cadaverous blue and swelled. The bare black earth gave off an inexpressibly sweet smell. Water bubbled in last year's wheel-tracks along the highroad. Fresh landslips yawned in the clayey ravines outside the village. A southerly wind brought the heavy scent of rotten grass from the Chir, and at midday delicate, pale-blue shadows could just be seen on the horizon, as in Spring. All over the village rippling pools stood by the ashes heaped up by the fences. The earth melted around the ricks on the threshing-floors, and the sickly-sweet smell of half-rotten straw pricked the noses of passers-by. In the daytime tarry water ran off the icicle-hung, straw roofs and cornices of the huts, the magpies chattered incessantly on the fences and the village bull, wintering in Miron Grigor'evich's yard, bellowed in the pangs of the premature languor of Spring. He tore at the fence with his horns and kicked up the crumbling, sodden snow in the yard.

The Don broke up on the second day of Christmas. The melting ice moved down the middle of the river with a mighty crunching and grinding. Like sleepy, monstrous fish the floes crawled out onto the banks. Across the Don, goaded by the agitating south wind, the poplars fled in immobile, billowing flight.

In this lush and often dramatic description of 'midwinter spring' on the Don the author is conveying the almost ineffable delight and uplift caused by the temporary relaxation of winter's grip. This is intimated through such expressions as *невыразимо сладкий запах; томлёные запахи; нежнейшие тени; приторная сладость; преждевременным томлением; волнующим ветром* and the rapid movement of the relatively simple syntax – the only conjunction used is *и*. The passage is structured around a process of accumulation to the climax of the moving of the ice – *с мощным хрустом* – on the Don.

The prose is dense with natural imagery, including such similes as *как ветер конскую гриву; как сонные чудовищные рыбы*, metaphors like *лёд, трупно синея; шалая неслась вода* and a profusion of details of the *Донская природа*, all conveyed in a concrete, highly sensuous vocabulary, appealing strongly to the senses of sight, smell and hearing, e.g. *зазеленели прошлогодняя травка и мшистые плитняки; трупно синея; сладкий запах; пузырилась вода; томлёные запахи; голубые, нежнейшие тени; приторная сладость; чечекали на плетнях сороки; с мощным хрустом и скрежетом.* The sense of particularity is heightened by Sholokhov's use of a huge number of vivid and precise nouns and adjectives, some of which are specialised, local words, e.g. *ерик; заедь; стор*, while the verbs are called upon to convey the sudden galvanisation of Nature, e.g. *шёл; неслась; стремились; вылезали; стекала; копытил; мотал.* This is reflected in the phraseology of the passage, which is vivid and evocative rather than striking or idiosyncratic in the expressionist manner of Bely or Babel' (qq.v.), e.g. the finely observed detail of *дубовую, изъеденную червоточиной соху* or *рыхлый, наъитанный талой водой снег.*

The introductory sentence is vividly dramatic in the implications of *заплетало* – as in a drama there is to be a rapid untying of knots by Time (hence *развязка*). However, these knots are strictly natural, as in a horse's mane, emphasised by the curt parallelism. In contrast the syntax of the next five paratactic clauses is inverted, thus rhythm and word-order emphasise the closely observed, visual details: *наступила оттепель; сутки шёл дождь; шалая неслась вода; травка и мшистые плитняки мела; пенились окраинцы.* The sudden reversion to a subject/complement word-order, and the striking metaphor, throw into relief a process, the results of which form the passage's climax – *лёд, трупно синея, вздувался.* The author then details some of the sights and smells resulting from the sudden thaw. Time and again he emphasises the quality of the processes set in motion by this 'midwinter spring', e.g. *невыразимо сладкий запах; томлёные запахи; нежнейшие тени; приторная сладость.* A distinctive rhythmic movement is imparted by the frequent multiple and detailed qualification of most nouns, e.g. *томлёные запахи травяного тлена; приторная сладость подопревшей соломы; по карнизам куреней с соломенных сосульчатых крыш стекала*, in each of which one cannot fail to notice rich assonance and alliteration. Moreover, the pace of events is briefly slowed down by the rather more static verbs almost hidden among the dense, lush phraseology: *зияли; маячили; стояли; колола в нос.*

The pace changes again as the great accumulation of detail from *днями* to *снег* conveys the simultaneity of the events recorded. Although the overall rhythmic effect of these two longest sentences in the passage (with their imperfective verbs recording actions in progress: *стекала; раскидывал; тёрся; мотал; копытил*) is different from that noted above, the constituent clauses (except one) are again paratactic. This gives great vigour to the bull's restlessness, while permitting the accumulation in one sentence of much precisely recorded detail.

Consequently, the final, climactic paragraph is all the more effective by contrast. The spareness in detail and brevity in rhythm of *На второй день рождества Дон взломало* draws the reader's attention to the sudden events on the river. Emphasis is placed on the details observed by repetition of similar devices: inversion of sentence elements with the subject in final position, thus creating an almost quadruple parallelism, and the qualification of nouns or verbs by vivid and resonant phraseology: *с мощным хрустом и скрежетом; как сонные, чудовищные рыбы; понукаемые южным волнующим ветром; в неподвижном зыбком беге.*

БОРИ́С ЛЕОНИ́́ДОВИЧ ПАСТЕРНА́К

(1890–1960)

Son of the painter Leonid Pasternak, Boris Pasternak grew up and spent most of his life in or near Moscow. His early interest in music owed much to the influence of his mother, a concert pianist, and the composer, Skriabin. He published his first volume of poetry in 1914, followed by the collections *Сестра́ моя́ жизнь* in 1922 and *Те́мы и вариа́ции* in 1923. Two epic poems, sympathetic to the revolutionary movement, *Девятьсо́т пя́тый год* and *Лейтена́нт Шмидт* both published in 1927, were followed by another collection of verse, *Второ́е рожде́ние*. Apart from two small wartime collections, *На ра́нних поезда́х* and *Земно́й просто́р*, he effectively fell silent as a poet until after Stalin's death, confining himself to translations of foreign literature, especially Shakespeare's plays and Georgian poetry. He began his 'desk-drawer' novel, *До́ктор Жива́го*, in 1946, but was obliged to publish it in Milan in 1957. In 1958 he was awarded the Nobel Prize for Literature, but was forced to decline it after many vicious verbal attacks on him by the Soviet authorities. His final volume of verse, *Когда́ разгуля́ется*, was published in Paris in 1959.

His early poetry, concerned with love, nature and poetic inspiration, though influenced by Blok and Mayakovsky (qq.v.), is highly original in imagery and diction, sometimes to the point of obscurity. In the latter half of his life his poetry moved away from modernism to the simplicity and clarity of the poems appended to *Doctor Zhivago*, one of which is printed below. Whatever its merits or demerits as a novel *per se*, *Doctor Zhivago* does emphasise Pasternak's prime concern with the spiritual integrity of the individual and those ideologies which threaten it.

121

Зимняя ночь

(1948)

1.   Мело, мело по всей земле
    Во все пределы.
    Свеча горела на столе,
    Свеча горела.

5.   Как летом роем мошкара
    Летит на пламя,
    Слетались хлопья со двора
    К оконной раме.

9.   Метель лепила на стекле
    Кружки и стрелы.
    Свеча горела на столе,
    Свеча горела.

13.   На озарённый потолок
    Ложились тени,
    Скрещенья рук, скрещенья ног,
    Судьбы скрещенья.

17.   И падали два башмачка
    Со стуком на пол.
    И воск слезами с ночника
    На платье капал.

21.   И всё терялось в снежной мгле
    Седой и белой.
    Свеча горела на столе,
    Свеча горела.

25.   На свечку дуло из угла,
    И жар соблазна
    Вздымал, как ангел, два крыла
    Крестообразно.

29.   Мело весь месяц в феврале,
    И то и дело
    Свеча горела на столе,
    Свеча горела.

A snow-storm swept over the whole earth,
From end to end.
The candle burned on the table,
The candle burned.

Like a swarm of midges in summer
Flying at a flame,
The snowflakes outside flew in swarms
Towards the window-frame.

The snow-storm modelled on the pane
Circles and arrows.
The candle burned on the table,
The candle burned.

On the brightly lit ceiling
Shadows fell:
Crossed hands, crossed legs,
Crossed destinies.

And two little shoes fell
To the floor with a thud.
And wax from the night-light
Dripped like tear-drops onto the dress.

And all was lost in the snowy gloom,
In the grey and white gloom.
The candle burned on the table,
The candle burned.

A draught from the corner blew at the candle,
And the heat of temptation,
Like an angel, raised two wings
In the shape of a cross.

The snow-storm lasted all February,
And continually   .
The candle burned on the table,
The candle burned.

This poem, which many consider primarily a love poem, can also be interpreted as a simple and forceful reflection of Pasternak's concern with the spiritual integrity of the individual, in that its 'candle' is a symbol of the human spirit unextinguished by the dark winter night of revolutions or social cataclysms. Despite the overall mood of gloom, the unfailing light of the candle implies an underlying sense of hope. Although it is variously assailed by forces symbolic of physical threat, chance, temptation and confusion, the candle is never extinguished, still burning triumphantly in the last line. Structurally, the poem is simple, but powerfully effective. The first stanza encapsulates the theme, presenting the two dominant images of the assailing snow-storm and the burning candle. The second, third and sixth stanzas develop and echo the first, while the last, albeit with slightly more detail, restates the theme. Within this overall structure, the equally threatening sub-themes of chance, disintegration, confusion and temptation are expressed in stanzas four to seven.

The persistence of all these phenomena finds its formal correspondence in eight stanzas of perfect, but not tedious, rhythmic and metrical regularity, each made up of an iambic tetrameter alternating with an iambic dimeter. The potential counterpoint of metrical and rhythmic stress is not at all exploited, but without detriment to the poem. Moreover, this regularity is syntactically reinforced by the fact that the poem's syntactic units usually comprise a couplet or an end-stopped line. Each stanza-quatrain is tightly controlled by a regular rhyme-scheme – *abab*, masculine and truncated feminine respectively.

Appropriately, the imagery of the poem is predominantly visual, exhibiting a Manichean contrast of light (the candle) and darkness (the snow-storm, darkness, blind forces). Despite its profundity of statement, the poem almost completely avoids abstract vocabulary, the exceptions being *судьба* and *соблазн*. Meaning is conveyed through a simple, concrete language, employing only two similes, with a striking predominance of nouns, the few verbs referring mainly to the candle or the snow-storm. This deceptive simplicity is elevated to the level of metaphor by incantatory repetition and a rich sound pattern.

From the first line one is struck by the incantatory repetition of *мело, всей/все* and *свеча горела*. The impersonal verb linked with *по всей земле/во все пределы* emphatically conveys the blind power of impersonal forces everywhere. This is further emphasised by stylistic means: absolute rhythmic regularity, the absence of punctuation at the end of l.1, the isolation of *свеча орела* in 1.4, and complex vowel and consonant alliteration, viz. *м/л/с/в* and stressed and unstressed *о/е/а*.

The second stanza presents more blind forces assailing the candle-flame, the snowflakes being likened to a swarm of midges threatening the flame. Typically, an idea is given 'a local habitation and a name' through the use of a metaphor from the natural world. The whole idea is succinctly expressed in a single sentence extending over a quatrain tightly bound by metre, rhythm and rhyme. As in the first stanza, Pasternak increases the impact of the verse with a subtle and varied sound pattern, in this case *к/л/м/р/с* and the vowels *а/о*.

Preceding the restatement of the 'refrain' is the representation of the snow-storm as almost a physical threat. The surprising *стрелы* is undoubtedly an echo of the Hamlet soliloquy ('To be or not to be ...') which plays a significant part in the novel and the appended poems. This stanza is given a particular fluidity by the abundance of the sounds *л/с/е*. Shadows of intimate moments cast by the candle-light lead the poet's thoughts in stanza 4 from a particular observation to one of the rare abstract elements in the poem, the elements of fate and chance which play an important part in the novel. Nevertheless, even the abstract *судьбы скрещенья* develops subtly from strong images of the imaginary shapes formed by the shadows. The phrase itself is given special emphasis by unexpected inversion. In this quatrain the sounds *с/к/н/р* play a major part. Unlike the fourth stanza the fifth is devoid of explicit abstraction, yet the ideas of the collapse of the familiar, intimate world experienced in social cataclysm and a concomitant grief are powerfully suggested by apparently insignificant events in the poet's room: a great deal is implied by the one word *слезами*. Yet again, sound pattern plays an important part, with its subtle interplay of *п/д/л/м/к/с* and the vowel sounds *а/и/э*.

Stanza 6 affords a strongly visual reprise of the basic theme, the greys and whites of the snowy gloom contrasting with the warmth of the candle-flame. Moreover, syntactical placing adds additional emphasis – *всё* receiving the first metric stress, and *седой и белой* placed after the noun in a line of their own. As in the third stanza the sounds *с* and *л* play a major role. The seventh stanza is somewhat obscure, consisting more of meaningful hints and an unusual interweaving of the concrete and the abstract. Syntactical prominence is given to *свечку*, now in diminutive form, the existence of which is threatened by the impersonal *дуло*. Without doubt there is religious significance in the presence of *ангел*, emphasised by the line-break after *вздымал*, and *крестообразно* which takes up a whole line. The precise significance of the isolated *жар соблазна* is not clear, yet obviously this sexual temptation is also seen as some form of spiritual event. In this rather obscure quatrain the complex interplay of vowel sounds is very striking, especially *a/o/y*.

The poem ends on a note of triumphant affirmation that, despite the prolonged threat of the snow-storm,

> *Свеча горела на столе,*
> *Свеча горела.*

ЮРИЙ ПА́ВЛОВИЧ КАЗАКО́В

(1927–   )

In his youth in Moscow he showed a talent for music and attended Music School. After completing secondary school (and having done his military service) he entered the Gor′ky Literary Institute, graduating in 1957. While still a student there, he worked on the newspaper, *Сове́тский спорт*, writing features on sports personalities. His first stories appeared in monthly journals in 1953. His first collection, *Ма́нька*, containing eleven stories including *А́рктур, – го́нчий пёс*, appeared in Archangel in 1958. Another collection, *На полуста́нке*, appeared in Moscow in 1959 containing twelve stories, four of them new ones. Between then and 1966 he published half-a-dozen new stories. Apart from a re-issue of stories under the title *О́сень в дубо́вых леса́х* in 1969 he has fallen silent, probably because of official attacks for insufficient contemporary social content, pessimism and passive, estranged heroes.

Kazakov is probably the best prose-writer of the fifties and sixties in the beauty and precision of his language, stylistic economy, emotional profundity and the poetic suggestiveness of his narratives. Most of his work is set in remote rural or North Russia, implicitly arguing their superiority over urban life, and deals with 'outsiders', whether it be plain girls, misanthropic cynics, rootless wanderers or the blind dog, Arcturus.

Арктур, – гончий пёс

(1958)

Но если не мог он ничего увидеть, зато в чутьё не могла с ним сравниться ни одна собака. Постепенно он изучил все запахи города и прекрасно ориентировался в нём. Не было случая, чтобы он заблудился и не нашёл дорогу домой. Каждая вещь пахла!

127

Запахов было множество, и все они звучали, все они громко заявляли о себе. Каждый предмет пах по-своему – одни неприятно, другие безлично, третьи сладостно. Стоило Арктуру поднять голову и понюхать в ту сторону, откуда тянул ветер, он сразу же ощущал свалки и помойки, дома, каменные и деревянные, заборы и сараи, людей, лошадей и птиц так же ясно, как будто видел всё это.

Был на берегу реки, за складами, большой серый камень, почти вросший в землю, который Арктур особенно любил обнюхивать. Камень сам по себе пах неинтересно, но в его трещинах и порах надолго задерживались самые удивительные и неожиданные запахи. Они держались подолгу, иной раз неделями, их мог выдуть только сильный ветер. Каждый раз, пробегая мимо этого камня, Арктур сворачивал к нему и долго занимался обследованием. Он фыркал, приходил в возбуждение, уходил и снова возвращался, чтобы выяснить себе допольнительную подробность.

И ещё он слышал тончайшие звуки, каких мы никогда не услышим. Он просыпался по ночам, раскрывал глаза, поднимал уши и слушал. Он слышал все шорохи за многие вёрсты вокруг. Он слышал пение комаров и зудение в осином гнезде на чердаке. Он слышал, как шуршит в саду мышь и тихо ходит кот по крыше сарая. И дом для него не был молчаливым и неживым, как для нас. Дом тоже жил: он скрипел, шуршал, потрескивал, вздрагивал чуть заметно от холода. По водосточной трубе стекала роса и, скапливаясь внизу, падала на плоский камень редкими каплями. Снизу доносился невнятный плеск воды в реке. Шевелился толстый слой брёвен в запани около лесозавода. Тихо поскрипывали уключины, – кто-то переплывал реку в лодке. И совсем далеко, в деревне, слабо кричали петухи по дворам. Это была жизнь, вовсе неведомая и неслышная нам, но знакомая и понятная ему.

But if he could see nothing, on the other hand there was no dog to compare with him for sense of smell. He had gradually learned all the town's smells and could find his way around in it splendidly. On no occasion did he get lost or fail to find his way home. Everything had a smell! There was a multitude of smells and all of them loudly and sonorously declared their presence. Every object had its own smell – some unpleasant, others characterless, others delightful. Arcturus only had to look up and sniff into the wind to sense immediately dumps and rubbish heaps, buildings – stone and wooden, fences and barns, people, horses and birds, just as well as if he could see them all.

On the river bank beyond the warehouses was a large, grey stone, almost buried in the ground, around which Arcturus was particularly fond of sniffing. The stone itself did not have a particularly interesting smell, but in its cracks and pores the most remarkable and unexpected smells remained for a long time. They hung on for ages, sometimes for weeks on end, and only a strong wind could dislodge them. Every time he passed this stone Arcturus would swing round to it and inspect it for a long time. He would snort, get excited, go away and come back again to clarify an additional detail.

He could also hear the slightest sounds which we could never hear. He would wake up at night, open his eyes, prick up his ears and listen. He could hear every rustle for miles around. He could hear the whine of mosquitoes and the buzzing in the wasps' nest in the attic. He could hear a mouse rustling and a cat walking quietly over the barn roof. Nor was the house silent and lifeless, as it is for us. The house was alive too: it squeaked, rustled, creaked and shuddered very slightly from the cold. Dew dripped down the down-spout and, collecting at the bottom, fell occasionally onto a flat stone. From below came the inaudible sound of the river lapping. A thick stack of logs was moving in the collecting-point near the timber-mill. Row-locks squeaked quietly, – somebody was rowing across the river. And far off, in the village, cocks were crowing faintly in the yards. This was a part of life completely unknown and inaudible to us, but familiar and comprehensible to him.

This passage describes how Arcturus' blindness was compensated for by the wonderful acuity of his sense of smell and hearing. To convince the reader (which he does) the narrator speaks in a voice of humble wonder and admiration, which is reflected in the diction and syntax, e.g. the use of strong contrasts: *Но если не мог он ничего увидеть, зато в чутьё не могла с ним сравниться ни одна собака; И ещё он слышал тончайшие звуки, каких мы никогда не услышим; Это была жизнь, вовсе неведомая и неслышная нам, но знакомая и понятная ему*; the use and frequency of such words as: *все; каждый; сразу же; так же ясно, как будто*; the use of superlatives; parataxis of clauses: *Он фыркал, приходил в возбуждение, уходил и снова возвращался; Он просыпался по ночам, раскрывал глаза, поднимал уши и слушал; он скрипел, шуршал, потрескивал, вздрагивал* ... The overall structure and development of the passage also serve to emphasise the dog's remarkable senses. The whole passage, unified by subject-matter and tone, develops from the general statement of the first sentence, the first paragraph providing typical examples, the second a specific instance. The final paragraph ascribes the same acuity to his hearing, ending with an echo of the first sentence – neither dogs nor men know what Arcturus knows.

The passage is dense with images of the world which Arcturus smelled and heard, from such generalisations as *запахов было множество* to such finely observed details as *тихо поскрипывали уключины*, conveyed in a simple, concrete and highly sensuous vocabulary – Kazakov has a rare ability in his evocation of the sights, smells and sounds of the material world. The great vigour and presence of Arcturus' world is transmitted by nouns and verbs in equal balance; Kazakov uses relatively few adjectives and adverbs so they tend to be all the more effective when used. Moreover, he has little recourse to striking phraseology, the nouns and verbs conveying their full meanings without unusual combinations.

The very first sentence amply conveys Kazakov's sensitivity for and skill in using the Russian language. The great effectiveness of this general statement results from a combination of extremely simple diction, the chiasmic contrast of the two clauses, and the word-order within the clauses themselves, i.e. the fluid movement of the first (especially because of the position of *он*) and the forceful inversions of the second. A similar sense of balance is evident in the second two-clause sentence, where the two adverbs are placed in parallel and at the head of their clauses for emphasis. It is at points like this that one senses the lessons of Kazakov's exemplar, Bunin (q.v.). The extent of Arcturus' knowledge is implied by the perfective verb *изучил* and the pronoun *все*.

The first two sentences syntactically typify this passage in another respect – Kazakov's eschewing complex hypotaxis and preferring limited subordination or none at all, and his employing parataxis of verbs and nouns. Strong negation is also used to emphasise the dog's capabilities – this is also the case in the following sentence: *Не было случая, чтобы он заблудился и не нашёл дорогу домой.* The sudden brevity of *каждая вещь пахла* and its leading adjective command attention, allowing the narrator to discourse generally about Arcturus' smelly world. Inversion announces these *запахи* and their large number, emphasised both by the paralleled *все они* and the evocative synaesthesia of *звучали, все они громко заявляли о себе.* The focus is narrowed down to *каждый предмет*; although Kazakov repeats the adjective he uses a different noun, setting up alliteration. Again he places elements in parallel, each contrasting with the other. The paragraph ends with an untypically long but syntactically very simple sentence. However, it is stylistically appropriate – the statement *Стоило Арктуру поднять голову и понюхать в ту сторону, откуда тянул ветер* with its typical two verbs *поднять* and *понюхать* is followed, in parataxis, by a great accumulation of objects, animate and inanimate, a universe of smells, while the adverbs *так же ясно* and the pronouns *всё это* emphasise the sureness of his sense of smell.

To illustrate Arcturus' experience of the world through smell Kazakov now focuses on a particular object, the great grey stone. The cumulative rhythm of the sentence elements, separated by punctuation, serves to place greater emphasis on the verb at the end (N.B. the implications of the prefix *об-*). By antithesis and a timely use of adjectives the stone's secrets are revealed: *камень* and *неинтересно* are placed initially and finally respectively with a minimal disturbance of word-order, whereas *но* announces antithesis and a complete inversion of word-order, placing *самые удивительные и неожиданные запахи* finally. These smells stayed and every time (*каждый* again) Arcturus was irresistibly attracted. His delight is splendidly and vigorously conveyed by a series of verbs almost in parataxis: *фыркал, приходил в возбуждение, уходил и снова возвращался* and the humorous *чтобы выяснить себе допольнительную подробность.*

The final paragraph extends this acuity to his hearing, emphasised by the superlative *тончайшие* and the strong negation. A typical instance is conveyed, as above, through a series of uncoordinated verbs. This device without doubt does impart great vigour and immediacy to his descriptions. The immense acuity of his hearing is emphasised by the incremental repetition of *он слышал* at the beginning of each sentence, but the nature of what he can hear is remarkably varied: *все шорохи; пение комаров; зудение в осиновом гнезде; шуршит мышь; тихо ходит кот.* The effect of such variety is increased by the syntactic variation of the predicates of *слышал* and a subtle (and so appropriate!) system of alliteration and assonance.

Contrast is again employed with reference to the house using, as in the second paragraph, two adjectives and, as in the first paragraph, brevity for effect: *дом тоже жил.* This brevity is expanded to the vigorous, musical parataxis of *скрипел, шуршал, потрескивал, вздрагивал.* Syntactically the following sentence is typical, but its system of assonance and alliteration is, as above, wonderfully appropriate. The last five sentences are, in contrast, brief and self-contained, emphasising each individual sound, each in a different way: *невнятный плеск; шевелился толстый слой; тихо поскрипывали; слабо кричали.* The exact parallelism and antithesis of the final sentence and the rare skill of the passage as a whole make this last statement completely credible.

ЕВГЕ́НИЙ АЛЕКСА́НДРОВИЧ ЕВТУШЕ́НКО

(1933–)

Born at Zima Station, near Irkutsk, of Ukrainian peasant stock, Yevtushenko openly proclaims his Siberian origins, considering a 'sibiryak' to be a tough, free frontiersman (despite Siberia's other claim to fame). His parents, however, belonged to the urban intelligentsia, and he himself spent the pre-war years in Moscow. Nevertheless, his stay from 1941 to 1944, as a war evacuee, in Siberia did provide him both with a background for many of his poems and a certain local colour in his poetic language. He returned to Moscow in 1944 and, despite a break in the mid-sixties, has lived there ever since. He describes himself as half-peasant and half-intellectual.

In 1948 he worked with his geologist father in the Altai region which provided the title for his first published volume of poems, *Разве́дчики грядущего* (1952). After this he managed to get a place in the official Soviet training-ground for writers, the Gor'ky Literary Institute. His best early work is the long poem, *Ста́нция Зима́* (1956), in which Yevtushenko writes not only about himself and his background but also about the moral consequences of Stalinism. From this point onwards he asserted the need for poetic honesty and integrity, especially concerning long-forbidden themes. This, coupled with a certain latter-day Futurist flamboyance, led to frequent critical attacks on him in the U.S.S.R. during the Khrushchov period and simultaneous acclaim from Soviet youth. The main volumes of this period were *Стихи́ ра́зных лет* (1959), *Взмах руки́* (1962) and the long poem, *Ба́бий яр* (1961), dealing with Soviet anti-Semitism.

Since 1960 he has travelled widely in the West and won a certain notoriety. The result of one such trip was the publication, originally in France, of *Autobiographie précoce* (1963), which caused much criticism in the U.S.S.R. because of its unorthodox interpretation of Soviet history. Yevtushenko's answer was silence and a refusal to participate in public 'debates' about the arts. A prolific poet, since then he has produced further volumes of poetry, including *Ка́тер свя́зи* (1966), *Иду́т бе́лые сне́ги* (1969), *Пою́щая да́мба* (1971– which includes the long half-poetry, half-prose '*Под ко́жей статуи свобо́ды*'), *Укра́денные я́блоки* (1971– a collection of his favourite verse of the last twenty years), *Отцо́вский слух* (1975) and *В по́лный рост* (1977), containing the long and tedious '*Ива́новские си́тцы*'. The latter poem shows where Yevtushenko's genius does *not* lie – he is a true poet in the brief, finely observed lyrics of the fifties and early sixties rather than the sprawling, turgid epics of the seventies.

Окно выходит в белые деревья

(1955)

Окно выходит в белые деревья.
Профессор долго смотрит на деревья.
Он очень долго смотрит на деревья
и очень долго мел крошит в руке.
5   Ведь это просто –
                правила деленья!
А он забыл их – правила деленья!
Забыл –
        подумать! –
               правила деленья.
Ошибка!
      Да!
           Ошибка на доске!
Мы все сидим сегодня по-другому.
10   И слушаем и смотрим по-другому,
да и нельзя сейчас не по-другому,
и нам подсказка в этом не нужна.
Ушла жена профессора из дому.
Не знаем мы,
           куда ушла из дому,

15 не знаем,
                    отчего ушла из дому,
    а знаем только,
                    что ушла она.
    В костюме и немодном и неновом,
    как и всегда немодном и неновом,
    да, как всегда немодном и неновом,
20 спускается профессор в гардероб.
    Он долго по карманам ищет номер:
    "Ну что такое?
                    Где же этот номер?
    Куда он делся? –
                    Трёт рукою лоб.
    Ах вот он! . . .
                Что ж,
                    как видно,
                            я старею.
25 Не спорьте, тётя Маша,
                        я старею.
    Ну что уж тут поделаешь –
                        старею . . ."
    Мы слышим –
                дверь внизу скрипит за ним.
    Окно выходит в белые деревья,
    в большие и красивые деревья,
30 но мы сейчас глядим не на деревья,
    мы молча на профессора глядим.
    Уходит он,
                сутулый,
                            неумелый,
    какой-то беззащитно неумелый,
    я бы сказал –
                устало неумелый,
35 под снегом, мягко падающим в тишь.
    Уже и сам он, как деревья, белый,
    да,
            как деревья,
                            совершенно белый,
    ещё немного –
                    и настолько белый,
39 что среди них его не разглядишь.

The window looks out onto white trees.
The professor stares at the trees,
for a long, long time stares at the trees,
crumbling chalk in his hand.
But they're easy
                    – the rules of division!
He's forgotten them – the rules of division!
Just think!
            Forgotten
                    the rules of division.
A mistake!
            Yes!
                    A mistake on the board!
Today we're all sitting differently,
looking and listening differently,
and right now it has to be differently,
we don't need any prompting.
The professor's wife's left home.
We don't know,
                    where she's gone,
we don't know,
                    why she's gone,
we just know,
                    she's gone.
In a suit not fashionable or new,
as always not fashionable or new,
yes, as always not fashionable or new,
the professor goes down to the cloakroom.
He looks and looks through his pockets for his number:
'What's happening?
                    Where *is* that number?
Perhaps,
        I didn't have a number?
What's happened to it? –
                    he rubs his forehead with his hand –
Ah, here it is! ...
                    Looks like I'm getting old.
Don't argue, Masha,
                    I'm getting old.
There's nothing for it –
                    I'm getting old ...'

We can hear
       the door squeak behind him.
The window looks out onto white trees,
onto big, beautiful trees,
but right now we're not watching trees,
in silence we're watching the professor.
Away he goes,
       round-shouldered,
            clumsy,
somehow helplessly clumsy,
I would say –
       tiredly clumsy,
in the snow, silently, softly falling.
Already, like the trees, he's white,
yes,
    like the trees,
         absolutely white,
a little later –
      so white
you cannot make him out.

The theme at the heart of this brief scene is the bond of
sympathy between different generations and compassion for
another's suffering. Appropriately the tone of the poem is a
sympathetic but solemn compassion, signalled both by incantatory repetition and certain adjectives: *и немодном и неновом*;
сутулый; *какой-то*; *неумелый*; certain adverbs: *очень долго*;
молча; *по-другому*; *беззащитно*; *мягко*; certain verbs: *старею*;
и что уж тут поделаешь; *скрипит* and certain phrases: *да и
нельзя сейчас*; *и нам подсказка в этом не нужна*; *мы все*.

    The poem's ideas are presented mainly by cumulative sug-
gestion, viz. the implications of: *долго . . . очень долго*; *мел
крошит*; *ведь забыл их*; *мы все*; *не нужна*; *знаем только*; *как и
всегда*; *он долго ищет*; *и что уж тут поделаешь – старею*; *не
на деревья*; *мы молча*; *настолько белый,/что среди них его не
разглядишь*.

    The absence of stanzas in this poem serves to emphasise the
brief dramatic narrative while, despite certain Mayakovskian
graphic devices, the end-stopped iambic pentameter lines
throughout slow down the pace and emphasise the sad dignity

of the situation. The striking rhyme-scheme (viz. *aaabaaabcccdcccd* ... etc.) gives a solemn incantatory effect, yet is varied by the new rhyme every fourth line.

The poem as a whole consists of a number of sensitively selected and progressively accumulating dramatic details of the professor's and the students' actions, and of his appearance. The vocabulary is simple, concrete and literal and quite devoid of figures of speech except the dominating anaphora (and the resultant alliteration). It is predominantly visual, thus heightening the dramatic effect. Moreover, its simplicity is appropriate to the sensitive and compassionate simplicity of tone. The poet employs adverbs in a special way, adding a certain intensity to whatever they qualify, e.g. *долго ... очень долго; да и нельзя; а знаем только; да, как всегда; молча; беззащитно; устало; совершенно; настолько.*

The spare descriptive phrase of the end-stopped first line is picked up and dramatised by the second and third, and given dramatic significance by the professor's preoccupation. The *долго* of the second line is picked up and intensified by *очень* in the third, enjambement of which heightens the poignancy of the fourth where the *очень долго* of the third line is echoed.

A similar device is employed in ll.5–8 and its effect is heightened by a graphic device to convey and emphasise the drama of the situation, and still further by the alliteration of *п/б/д*. The students' attitude to the professor's grief is succinctly conveyed by a single *все* and the verbs *сидим; слушаем; смотрим* with their strong alliteration. The device in 1.1 of the single end-stopped line subsequently amplified is also used in 1.9.

Line 13 with its significant inversion: *Ушла жена профессора из дому* and the students' attitude to the fact is emphasised by a graphic caesura and alliterative *м* and *а*. The significant words *куда; отчего* and *только* are pointed out by this device. The adjectives *и немодном и неновом* are emphasised by their position *after* the noun and given dramatic significance by the adverbial phrases *как и всегда; да, как и всегда*. The placing of the line *спускается профессор в гардероб* as the last of four lines provides an element of surprise.

The professor's confusion is brought out by the repetition of *номер* and dramatically heightened by the graphic device. The verb *старею* is given great poignancy by its progressive isolation. Unlike the first three lines the *деревья* of ll.28–31 are employed in a different way – they are no longer the object of attention, because the professor has replaced them as a significant object outside. The *молча* of l.31 has a tremendously poignant and sympathetic compassion. Similarly pregnant with meaning are the adjectives and adverbs *сутулый; неумелый; какой-то беззащитно неумелый; устало неумелый*. The solemn silence of the class is heightened by the pathetic fallacy of *в тишь*. The whole poem is rounded off by the professor merging into the white trees at which he was looking in the first line.

АЛЕКСА́НДР ИСА́ЕВИЧ СОЛЖЕНИ́ЦЫН

(1918–)

Born into a relatively poor family in Kislovodsk in the North Caucasus, Solzhenitsyn moved with his widowed mother to Rostov-on-Don in 1924. On leaving school in 1936 he already wished to be a writer but, lacking the means to go to Moscow and not wishing to leave his mother, entered Rostov University to read mathematics and physics. Despite his literary preferences he graduated with merit in 1941. Meanwhile, he had won a Stalin scholarship to enrol for a correspondence course at the Institute of Philosophy, Literature and History in Moscow, which he also successfully completed in 1941.

In the same year he took up a post as a physics teacher in a secondary school in Morozovka in the Rostov region, but was called up within a month. After a one-year course in artillery school he received a commission in 1942. He was sent to Leningrad where he served until February 1945, a twice decorated captain. In that month he was suddenly arrested for criticising Stalin in his letters. In July he was sentenced to eight years' hard labour, at first near Moscow and later in central Kazakhstan, where he contracted cancer. He was released in the same month as Stalin's death in 1953, but had to remain in Kazakhstan in administrative exile, teaching mathematics and physics. Rehabilitated in 1956 he eventually settled in Ryazan'.

He completed *Оди́н день Ива́на Дени́совича* in 1958, but did not send it to *Но́вый мир* until 1961. Thanks to Khrushchov himself it was published in the magazine in November 1962, an instant success. Its fame is due both to its being the first really authentic account of life in a Soviet labour camp, with its moral significance, and to its high artistic merit. Three more stories, *Матрёнин двор*, *Слу́чай на ста́нции Кречето́вка* and *Для по́льзы де́ла*, were published in 1963. After the fall of Khrushchov in 1964 Solzhenitsyn fell rapidly out of favour. Having written a long critical letter to the Fourth Congress of the Union of Soviet Writers in 1967 and having committed the heinous crime of having his two major novels, *Ра́ковый ко́рпус* and *В пе́рвом кругу́*, published in the West in 1968, he was expelled from the Writers' Union in 1969. He fell increasingly foul of the authorities, especially after his being awarded the Nobel Prize in 1970 which, unlike Sholokhov (q.v.), he was not allowed to collect. His third novel, *А́вгуст 14-ого*, rejected by Soviet publishing houses, was published in Paris in 1971. His anti-Soviet, anti-Western Slavophile views were made clear in his lecture composed for the Nobel Prize ceremony, published in Stockholm in August 1972. Expelled from the Soviet Union in 1974 he has since occupied himself with the semi-documentary *Архипела́г гула́г, 1918–56*, a projected seven-part study of the Soviet prison- and labour-camp system. Assessment of his qualities as a writer is complicated by his anti-Soviet stance. In the West, he has either been hailed as a patriarchal, Slavophile genius or dismissed as naive, arrogant and tiresomely prolix.

Один день Ивана Денисовича

(1962)

Потом, глядя на беленький-беленький чепчик Вдовушкина, Шухов вспомнил медсанбат на реке Ловать, как он пришёл туда с повреждённой челюстью и – недотыка ж хренова! – доброй волею в строй вернулся. А мог пяток дней полежать.

Теперь вот грезится: заболеть бы недельки на две, на три не насмерть и без операции, но чтобы в больничку положили, – лежал бы, кажется, три недели, не шевельнулся, а уж кормят бульоном пустым – лады. Но, вспомнил Шухов, теперь и в больничке отлежу нет. С каким-то этапом новый доктор появился – Степан Григорьевич, гонкий такой да звонкий, сам смутится, и больным нет покою: выдумал всех ходячих больных выгонять на работу при больнице: загородку городить, дорожки делать, на клумбы землю нанашивать, а зимой – снегозадержание. Говорит, от болезни работа – первое лекарство.

От работы лошади дохнут. Это понимать надо. Ухайдакался бы сам на каменной кладке – небось бы тихо сидел.

... А Вдовушкин писал своё. Он, вправду, занимался работой 'левой', но для Шухова непостижимой. Он переписывал новое

длинное стихотворение, которое вчера отделал, а сегодня обещал
показать Степану Григорьевичу, тому самому врачу, поборнику
трудотерапии.

Как это делается только в лагерях, Степан Григорьевич и
посоветовал Вдовушкину объявиться фельдшером, поставил его
на работу фельдшером, и стал Вдовушкин учиться делать
внутривенные уколы на тёмных работягах, в чью
добропорядочную голову никак бы не могло вступить, что
фельдшер может быть вовсе и не фельдшером. Был же Коля
студент литературного факультета, арестованный со второго
курса. Степан Григорьевич хотел, чтоб он написал в тюрьме то,
чего ему не дали на воле.

Then, while looking at Vdovushkin's oh-so-white little cap,
Shukhov remembered the medical battalion on the Lovat'
river, how he'd gone there with a busted jaw and – what a
bloody fool! – had returned of his own free will to his regiment.
And he could have stayed in for nearly a week.

Here he was dreaming – wouldn't it be nice to fall sick for a
couple of weeks or so, not so bad they'd have to operate, but
enough to get put in the infirmary – he'd stay there, he
reckoned, for three weeks, wouldn't stir, and they'd be feeding
him on that clear soup – not bad! But, Shukhov remembered,
there was no staying in bed in the infirmary now. A new doctor
had appeared with the latest lot – Stepan Grigor'evich he was
called, a fussy loud-mouth, gave himself no rest nor the
patients: he had thought up driving out all patients who could
walk to work round the hospital: putting up fences, making
paths, carrying earth for the flower-beds and, in winter, snow-
retention. Work, he said, was a first-rate medicine for illness.

Work'll kill horses. He ought to know that. If he was
working himself to death on the building site, he'd quieten
down, you could be sure of that.

... Vdovushkin went on with his writing. He was in reality
doing some work 'on the side', but it was incomprehensible to
Shukhov. He was copying out a new long poem which he had
finished off the day before, and had promised to show it today
to Stepan Grigor'evich, the very same doctor who advocated
work-therapy.

As can happen only in the camps, Stepan Grigor'evich had
advised Vdovushkin to declare himself to be a medical assist-

ant, had taken him on as such, and Vdovushkin had begun learning to give intravenous injections to ignorant prisoners to whose innocent minds it would never occur that a medical assistant could be other than a medical assistant. Kolya had in fact been a university student of literature, arrested in his second year. Stepan Grigor'evich wanted him to write in prison what he had not been allowed to write while free.

Two third-person narrative voices describe Shukhov's wish to report sick being thwarted by the harsh new doctor Stepan Grigor'evich, who is nevertheless showing considerable favouritism to the former student and writer, Kolya Vdovush-kin. In this extract, as elsewhere in the book, there are two narrative voices – the omniscient author and the зек Shukhov, the former reporting events in largely literary Russian, the latter in a mixture of rural speech and prison argot. The transition from one to the other involves subtle lexical, syntactical and tonal shifts. Shukhov's reported interior monologue introduces the passage and extends to *нет покою*. Typical of him are *А мог пяток дней полежать* in its piqued tone, curt ellipsis and use of diminutive; the sudden interjection *недотыка ж хренова!*; the particles and dialect afterthought in *а уж кормят бульоном пустым – лады*. The omniscient narrator's voice is apparent in the last paragraph, reflected in the irony and greater lexical and syntactical complexity of *в чью добропорядочную голову никак бы не могло вступить, что фельдшер может быть вовсе и не фельдшером.*

   This narrative technique, developed by the fabulist and author of the now bowdlerised *Толко́вый Слова́рь великору́сского словаря́* (1861–8), V. I. Dal' (d. 1872), and perfected by Leskov, is known as *сказ*. It was brought back into vogue by Remizov in the early twentieth century and enjoyed great popularity with such writers as Pil'nyak, Zamyatin and Babel' (qq.v.), especially because of the great importance ascribed to it by the Formalist critics of that time. Its value is its endowing narration with a double viewpoint, that of the omniscient, literate narrator and that of the semi-literate but 'on the spot' popular narrator. Consequently, the very structure of the passage is one of subtle transitions, not necessarily graphically marked by the paragraph. Shukhov's wishes and pique at the new doctor extend to roughly half-way through the third paragraph, the remainder of which consists of the omniscient narrator's explanations. From *От работы* to *тихо сидел* is again Shukhov's interior monologue. In the rest of the passage the omniscient narrator explains Stepan Grigor′evich's favouritism towards Kolya Vdovushkin. Such a narrative technique, of course, involves the use of an unusually wide lexical range from the simple and concrete to the elaborate and abstract. Thus, in Shukhov's interior monologue we find *беленький-беленький; недотыка ж хренова!; больничка; лады; ухайдакался,* whereas in the omniscient narrator's descriptions and commentary we find *непостижимой; поборнику трудотерапии; внутривенные уколы; добропорядочную голову.*

The progress of the narrative in this passage, as elsewhere in the book, involves almost imperceptible changes. The viewpoint probably changes between the literary gerund *глядя* and the diminutives and reduplicative *беленький-беленький чепчик.* This is confirmed by the stump-compound *медсанбат,* the parenthetic and slangy expletive *недотыка ж хренова!,* and the diminutive *пяток дней.* Lexically this continues to the popular genitive form *покою.* Moreover, this section is marked by the ellipsis and parataxis typical of popular Russian speech. The omniscient narrator briefly and impersonally intercedes to explain after the colon – his presence is signalled by his use of *ходячих* and *снегозадержание,* the absence of slang or colloquialisms, the controlled parallelism of *загородку городить, дорожки делать, на клумбы землю нанашивать,* and the impersonal tone.

Shukhov then intervenes to comment on Stepan Grigor′evich's reported aphorism with his own peasant aphorism *От работы лошади дохнут.* His presence is lexically and syntactically very obvious in *Ухайдакался бы сам на каменной кладке – небось бы тихо сидел.*

The final two paragraphs show a lexical transition back to the omniscient narrator – here standard literary Russian is used and, with the exception of *тёмных работягах,* slang and colloquialisms are avoided. Moreover, the syntactical structures are markedly different. In the penultimate paragraph the word-order is the standard subject/verb/non-verbal predicate, extended by a carefully balanced co-ordination, e.g. *но для Шухова непостижимой* and *которое вчера отделал, а сегодня обещал показать Степану Григорьевичу, тому самому врачу, поборнику трудотерапии*. In the final paragraph, only an omniscient, literate narrator could generalise to the following extent: *как это делается только в лагерях*, and employ such complex syntax and irony as that exhibited in the section from *как это* to *не фельдшером*. The final two sentences show the same features, especially the precise parallelism of *чтоб он написал в тюрьме то, чего ему не дали на воле*.

SOVIET POLITICAL PROSE

The following is an extract from a book on chess (sic!) in the U.S.S.R., published in 1956. Its style is typical of most Soviet political prose published since the late 1920s. The features noted in the following analysis are to be found with little variation in any copy of *Правда* or *Известия*.

В славные дни Октября 1917 года руководимые Коммунистической партией трудящиеся массы России взяли власть в свои руки и стали строить социализм. Это событие имеет всемирно-историческое значение. Оно явилось поворотным пунктом в истории человечества.

Бессмертный подвиг Коммунистической партии и рабочего класса России вдохновил трудящихся капиталистических стран на усиление борьбы против капиталистов, а угнетённые народы Востока – на борьбу против колониального гнёта. По примеру России, трудящиеся массы ряда капиталистических государств свергли капиталистов и успешно строят социализм. Многие колониальные народы уже добились национальной независимости и борются за построение справедливого общества. Рождённый Великим Октябрём, непрерывно рос и мужал лагерь социализма. Сейчас он представляет собой сплочённую, самую прогрессивную, самую передовую силу человечества.

Ничто и никто не может остановить могучую поступь нового мира, мира социализма. Он приковывает к себе взоры трудящихся всех стран, вселяет веру в лучшее будущее человечества. Миролюбивая внешняя политика Советского Союза, Китайской Народной Республики и стран народной демократии встречает поддержку и сочувствие всех передовых людей.

Вместе с советским народом всё прогрессивное человечество отмечает 39-ю годовщину коренного поворота в мировой истории от капиталистического общества к социализму, годовщину

велиκой Октябрьской социалистической революции. В этот
торжественный день советский народ отмечает свои успехи в
хозяйственном и культурном строительстве, демонстрирует свою
непреклонную волю сохранить мир во всём мире.

За 39 лет советской власти из аграрной страны с отсталой
техникой наша Родина превратилась в передовую
индустриальную державу. Вырос и возмужал советский человек,
активный и сознательный строитель коммунистического
общества. Радостно сознавать нашему народу, что своим
беззаветным трудом он создал всё, чем может гордиться наша
страна.

Современный этап развития советского общества
характеризуется невиданным взлётом творческой энергии народа,
новым мощным подъёмом его политической и производительной
активности.

In the glorious days of October 1917 the working people of
Russia, led by the Communist Party, took power into their own
hands and began to build socialism. This was an event of great
significance in the history of the world, a turning point in the
history of humanity.

The immortal feat of the Communist Party and the Russian
working class inspired the workers of the capitalist countries to
step up the struggle against the capitalists, and the oppressed
peoples of the East against the yoke of colonialism. Following
Russia's example the workers of a number of capitalist states
have overthrown the capitalists and are now building socialism.
Many colonial peoples have already achieved national inde-
pendence and are struggling to build a just society. The socialist camp, born of Great October, has grown and matured
without interruption. It now constitutes a united force, the
most advanced and progressive in humanity.

Nothing and nobody can stop the mighty advance of the new
world, the world of socialism. The gaze of the workers of all
countries is riveted on it; it inspires faith in a better future for
humanity. The peace-loving foreign policy of the Soviet Union,
the People's Republic of China and the People's Democracies
meets with the support and sympathy of all progressive people.

Along with the Soviet people all progressive humanity is
celebrating the 39th anniversary of a turning-point in the
history of the world – from capitalist society to socialism – the

anniversary of the Great October Socialist Revolution. On thi
solemn day the Soviet people is celebrating its successes i
economic and cultural construction and demonstrating it
unbending desire to preserve peace throughout the world.

In the 39 years of Soviet power our Motherland has change
from a backward agricultural country into an advanced indus
trial power. Soviet Man, the active and politically consciou
builder of Communist society, has grown and is still maturing
Our people can feel glad that by their selfless efforts they hav
created everything our country can feel proud of.

The present stage in the development of Soviet society i
characterised by an unprecedented upsurge of popular creativ
energy and a powerful new advance in political and productiv
activity.

The theme of this passage is the historico-political significanc
of the October Revolution on its 39th anniversary, both to th
Soviet Union and to other countries. This type of prose coul
be called expository-oratorical because, while communicatin
information, it also arouses feeling.

The tone of this and countless similar passages is ver
striking. It is a combination of a categorical, assertiv
enthusiasm with an almost religious elation. The tone is signal
led in particular by a very distinctive feature, viz. the use o
emotionally coloured adjectives and nouns, e.g. *славные
бессмертный подвиг; рождённый Великим Октябрём; самую
могучую поступь; торжественный; наша Родина; радостно
беззаветным трудом; невиданным взлётом.*

Its structure is one of logical development appropriate t
expository prose. This development proceeds on the followin
lines: the October Revolution – its effect on the rest of th
world – socialism's inevitable victory – the 39th anniversary o
the October Revolution – the development of the Soviet Unio
in the course of 39 years, i.e. from the particular to the general
viz. the Revolution and generalisations about it. The content
of the whole piece are unified by the great event of 1917.

It is almost self-evident to say that this prose has no artisti
merit, not because of its political content, since this in itsel
does not perforce vitiate good style, but because the language
is not used creatively; it is a mere permutation of clichés.

There is a limited but distinctively idiosyncratic use o

imagery in this passage, namely a series of dead metaphors betraying the writer's attitude to his material, e.g. *подвиг; вздохновил; гнёта; рождённый; могучую поступь; приковывает к себе взоры; вырос и возмужал; взлётом.* The emotions aroused by this passage find their expression in its elaborate, figurative and abstract vocabulary. It is to be noted that many of its abstract nouns are peculiar to the writer's conception of history. A striking aspect of this vocabulary is its adjectives – of an abstract and highly emotional nature, e.g. *беззаветным; славные; бессмертный; могучую; непреклонную.* Very revealing of the writer's assumptions, or rather presumptions, is the use – five times – of the pronoun *все.*

Probably the most striking feature of 'Sovietese' (i.e. that style of written Russian peculiar to political texts of the Soviet period) is its phraseology, which betrays its partisan, emotional attitude. There are obvious similarities between it and the language of the dogmatic religions. Just as a Catholic, when speaking of Christ, will say 'Our Lord', the writer of 'Sovietese' will only speak of the Bolshevik Revolution as the *Великая Октябрьская социалистическая революция.* This passage has many examples of such 'dogmatic' phraseology, e.g. *славные дни; руководимые Коммунистической партией; трудящиеся массы; всемирно-историческое; бессмертный подвиг; Великим Октябрём; непрерывно; самую; ничто и никто не может; могучую поступь; веру в лучшее будущее; миролюбивая внешняя политика; Великой Октябрьской социалистической революции; торжественный день; непреклонную волю; наша Родина.*

Inevitably such obligatory, yet cumbersome phraseology must affect the rhythm of Soviet political prose. In the first paragraph the first sentence presents a striking contrast to the two subsequent paratactic ones. The subject, an obligatory cliché, completely alters the rhythm of four otherwise simple statements. Obviously the writer's primary concern was not a pleasing prose rhythm. The second large paragraph structurally consists of a series of simple paratactic clauses, but each with its own peculiar rhythm, viz. a complex subject/a single verb/a complex object (with some variations in balance), e.g. *Бессмертный подвиг Коммунистической партии и рабочего класса России вздохновил трудящихся капиталистических стран на усиление борьбы против капиталистов.* Another

example of this is to be found in the third paragraph: *Миро-*
любивая внешняя политика Советского Союза, Китайской
Народной Республики и стран народной демократии
встречает поддержку и сочувствие всех передовых людей.
Consequently sentence length is artificially increased by
'obligatory' dogmatic phraseology. The resultant lumbering
rhythm might be graphically represented as follows: (————)
(–) (————). The general result is that the fundamentally
simple rhythm of the Russian sentence has been artificially
extended and distorted to a grotesque imbalance.

PART II

Passages for Explication

А. А. АХМÁТОВА

Был он ревнивым, тревожным и нежным,
Как Божье солнце, меня любил,
А чтобы она не запела о прежнем,
Он белую птицу мою убил.

Промолвил, войдя на закате в светлицу:
'Люби меня, смейся, пиши стихи!'
И я закопала весёлую птицу
За круглым колодцем у старой ольхи.

Ему обещала, что плакать не буду,
Но каменным сделалось сердце моё,
И кажется, что всегда и повсюду
Услышу я сладостный голос её.

(Осень 1914)

What is the *белая птица*, and what is the writer's attitude to it?
What are the contributions, if any, of stanza form, metric system and rhyme?
What is the nature of the reality evoked and what kind of vocabulary is employed in the evocation?
Consider the role of pronouns, adjectives and adverbs in this poem.
Is the sound pattern of any significance?

Н. М. КАРАМЗИ́Н –
Бедная Лиза

(1792)

Часто прихожу на сиё место и почти всегда встречаю там весну; туда же прихожу и в мрачные дни осени горевать вместе с природою. Страшно воют ветры в стенах опустевшего монастыря, между гробов, заросших высокою травою, и в тёмных переходах келий. Там, опёршись на развалины гробных камней, внимаю глухому стону времён, бездною минувшего поглощённых, – стону, от которого сердце моё содрогается и трепещет. Иногда вхожу в келии и представляю себе тех, которые в них жили, – печальные картины! Здесь вижу седого старца, преклонившего колена перед распятием и молящегося о скором разрешении земных оков своих, ибо все удовольствия исчезли для него в жизни, все чувства его умерли, кроме чувства болезни и слабости. Там юный монах – с бледным лицом, с томным взором – смотрит в поле сквозь решётку окна, видит весёлых птичек, свободно плавающих в море воздуха, видит – и проливает горькие слёзы из глаз своих. Он томится, вянет, сохнет – и унылый звон колокола возвещает мне безвременную смерть его.

Having determined the theme of the passage, ascertain its all-important tone and show how this determines the passage's structure, diction and syntax.
What similarities in style do you detect in this extract and Goldsmith's *Vicar of Wakefield* and Sterne's *Sentimental Journey*?

М. А. ВОЛÓШИН

Облака клубятся в безднах зелёных
    Лучезарных пустынь восхода,
И сбегают тени с гор обнажённых
    Цвета роз и мёда.

И звенит и блещет белый стеклярус
    За Киик-Атламой костистой,
Плещет в синем ветре дымчатый парус,
    Млеет след струистый.

Отливают волны розовым глянцем,
    Влажные выгибая гребни,
Индевеет берег солью и сланцем,
    И алеют щебни.

Скрыты горы синью пятен и линий –
    Переливами перламутра . . .
Точно кисть лиловых бледных глициний,
    Расцветает утро.

(1910)

Киик-Атламой – Kiik-Atlama, a mountainous cape on the Black Sea near Koktebel'.

What features does this poem share with contemporary French painting (Voloshin lived in Paris for many years and studied painting there) and to what extent do they make it a striking evocation of a Crimean dawn?
What other formal elements contribute to the two-dimensional pictorial quality of this poem?

А. Г. БИ́ТОВ –

Жены нет дома

(1963)

Значит, я никуда не ходил, думаю. Она приходит, а я сижу в прибранной комнате и занимаюсь. Спокоен и холоден . . .

Актёрка . . .

И я очень спешу пообедать и немного прибраться.

Успеваю.

Сижу. Актёрка . . .

В учебнике неинтересно.

Завалилась, наверно, в кабак . . . Вот она приходит пьяная. А я ей разогреваю обед, укладываю спать . . .

И ничего ей не говорю. А наутро у неё угрызения . . . Но я ей ничего не говорю.

Лучше лечь в постель. Буду лежать и читать учебник.

Лежу. Акт7рка . . .

А может, она шла пьяная – или даже лучше трезвая, – и ей отрезало ноги. Но я от неё не отказываюсь. Я ничего не даю ей почувствовать. Мы даже стали дружнее. Вот как та пара, что ходит по нашей улице: он седой и красивый, а она красивая и без ног . . .

Лежу.

Наконец-то!

Я вскакиваю как ошпаренный, впрыгиваю в халат . . . Невозмутимо открываю дверь, не говорю ей ни слова и хладнокровно ложусь обратно. Лицом к стене.

Discuss Bitov's unusual (for Soviet literature) narrative technique with reference to the speaker's tone and the structure of the monologue.

How does the use of language and syntax convey the narrator's 'stream of consciousness'?

А. К. ТОЛСТО́Й

Вновь растворилась дверь на влажное крыльцо,
В полуденных лучах следы недавней стужи
Дымятся. Тёплый ветер повеял нам в лицо
И морщит на полях синеющие лужи.

Ещё трещит камин, отливами огня
Минувший тесный мир зимы напоминая,
Но жаворонок там, над озимью звеня,
Сегодня возвестил, что жизнь пришла иная.

И в воздухе звучат слова, не знаю чьи,
Про счастье, и любовь, и юность, и доверье,
И громко вторят им бегущие ручьи,
Колебля тростника желтеющие перья.

Пускай же как они по глине и песку
Растаявших снегов журча уносят воды,
Бесследно унесёт души твоей тоску
Врачующая власть воскреснувшей природы!

(1870)

How does Tolstoy create a strong, memorable poem from a relatively trivial pathetic fallacy?

А. С. ПУ́ШКИН –
Выстрел
(1831)

Это было на рассвете. Я стоял на назначенном месте с моими тремя секундантами. С неизъяснимым нетерпением ожидал я моего противника. Весеннее солнце взошло, и жар уже наспевал. Я увидал его издали. Он шёл пешком, с мундиром на сабле, сопровождаемый одним секундантом. Мы пошли к ним нарстречу. Он приблизился, держа фуражку, наполненную черешнями. Секунданты отмерили нам двенадцать шагов. Мне должно было стрелять первому, но волнение злобы во мне было столь сильно, что я не понадеялся на верность руки и, чтобы дать себе время остыть, уступал ему первый выстрел; противник мой не соглашался. Положили бросить жребий: первый номер достался ему, вечному любимцу счастия. Он прицелился и прострелил мне фуражку. Очередь была за мною. Жизнь его наконец была в моих руках; я глядел на него жадно, стараясь уловить хотя одну тень беспокойства . . . Он стоял под пистолетом, выбирая из фуражки спелые черешни и выплёвывая косточки, которые долетали до меня. Его равнодушие взбесило меня. Что пользы мне, подумал я, лишить его жизни, когда он ею вовсе не дорожит? Злобная мысль мелькнула в уме моём. Я опустил пистолет. 'Вам, кажется, теперь не до смерти, – сказал я ему, – вы изволите завтракать: мне не хочется вам помешать.' – 'Вы ничуть не мешаете мне, – возразил он, – извольте себе стрелять, а впрочем как вам угодно; выстрел ваш остаётся за вами; я всегда готов к вашим услугам.' Я обратился к секундантам, объявив, что нынче стрелять не намерен, и поединок тем и кончился.

Having made a detailed explication of this passage, how would you describe Pushkin's prose style?

Do you consider it an appropriate vehicle for the subject-matter?

Do you see any differences from or similarities to the extract from *Медный всадник*?

И. Ф. А́ННЕНСКИЙ –
Тоска кануна

(1904)

О, тусклость мёртвого заката,
Неслышной жизни маята,
Роса цветов без аромата,
Ночей бессонных духота.

Чего-чего, канун свиданья,
От нас надменно ты не брал,
Томим горячкой ожиданья,
Каких я благ не презирал?

И, изменяя равнодушно
Искусству, долгу, сам себе,
Каких уступок, малодушный,
Не делал, Завтра, я тебе?

А для чего все эти муки
С проклятьем медленных часов? . . .
Иль в миге встречи нет разлуки,
Иль фальши нет в эмфазе слов?

маята – маета

What is the poet's attitude to his theme, and how is the theme
developed?

Consider the relative frequency and contribution of nouns,
adjectives and verbs in this poem.

How would you describe Annensky's diction?

To what extent does he exploit a possible counterpoint of
underlying rhythm and imposed metrical form, and to what
effect?

Н. А. ОСТРÓВСКИЙ –

Рождённые бурей

(1936)

Андрий узнал об опасности, лишь когда в окно грянул выстрел и пуля свистнула у его головы. Он невольно выпустил кольцо. Рёв смолк. Спасаясь от нового выстрела, Андрий бросился к угольной яме.

Вытянув руки с карабином вперёд, в окно втискивался легионер. Сзади его подталкивали. Тогда Андрий схватил кусок антрацита и, рискуя быть убитым, выскочил из ямы. Размахнулся, с силой швырнул углем в окно и попал в лицо легионера. Тот взвыл. Лицо его вмиг окровавилось. Он уронил карабин и повалился на руки державших его снизу охранников. Карабин лязгнул о цементный пол котельной. Вновь бабахнул выстрел. Андрий ошалел от радости. Он бомбардировал окно каменным углем. За окном послышались дикие ругательства. Люди с лестницы поспешно сползли на землю.

Андрия охватило неистовство. Он отстегнул свой пояс и привязал им кольцо к регулятору давления. Гудок вновь зарычал. Уже не прерывисто, так как Птаха прикрепил ремень наглухо.

Теперь руки Андрия были свободны. Боясь быть застигнутым врасплох, он непрерывно швырял углем в окно.

В пылу борьбы Птаха забыл, что в котельной есть ещё два окна. Только когда из обоих нераскрытых окон вылетели стёкла и со стен посыпалась штукатурка, Андрий с тоской понял, что с тремя окнами ему не справиться. Пули опять загнали его в угольную яму. В одном из окон появилось дуло карабина.

Андрий – Ukrainian form of *Андрей*
легионер – *Польский солдат*

A dupe of Soviet mythopoeia, the writer Nikolay Ostrovsky rarely rose above mediocrity. However, in his second, unfinished novel he showed an awareness that political merit alone was not sufficient to justify commendation and accordingly attempted to improve his style. The above extract contains some of the best prose he ever wrote. Write an appreciation of it and comment on its merits, if you consider it has any.

К. Д. БАЛЬМО́НТ –
Исландия
(1899)

Валуны и равнины, залитые лавой,
Сонмы глетчеров, брызги горячих ключей.
Скалы, полные грусти своей величавой,
Убелённые холодом бледных лучей.

Тени чахлых деревьев и море . . . О, море!
Волны, пена и чайки, пустыня воды!
Здесь забытые скальды на влажном просторе
Пели песни при свете вечерней звезды.

Эти Снорри, Сигурды, Тормодды, Гуннары
С именами железными, духи морей,
От ветров получили суровые чары
Для угрюмой, томительной песни своей.

И в строках перепевных доныне хранится
Ропот бури, и гром, и ворчанье волны, –
В них кричит альбатрос, длиннокрылая птица,
Из воздушной, из мёртвой, из вольной страны.

Снорри – Snorri Sturluson, the thirteenth-century author of the 'Younger Edda'.
Тормодды – Þormóðr, the thirteenth-century author of the 'Fóstbrœðra Saga'.
Сигурды . . . Гуннары – Sigurðr and Gunarr, heroes of the Sagas and Eddas.
альбатрос – a poetic licence, since the albatross is rarely found in the Northern Hemisphere.

Having completed your appreciation, what aspects of the poem do you think led Bryusov (q.v.) to write the following about it?: '*К. Д. Бальмонт много путешествовал, изъездил весь мир, был в Египте, в Мексике, на Тихом море и ещё во многих других местах. Все земли, где он побывал, Бальмонт описывал в стихах и в прозе. Но живее всего он описал страну, в которой никогда не был, – Исландию . . .*'

163

В. Ф. ТЕНДРЯКÓВ –
Ухабы

(1956)

Ох, дорога! – каждый метр с боя.

Вася Дергачёв хорошо знал её капризы. Эту лужу, на вид мелкую, безобидную, с торчащими из кофейной воды бугристыми хребтами глины, нельзя брать с разгона. В неё нужно мягко, бережно, как ребёнка в тёплую ванну, спустить машину, проехать с нежностью. На развороченный вкривь и вкось, со вздыбленными рваными волнами густо замешанной грязи кусок дороги следует набрасываться с яростным разгоном, иначе застрянешь на середине, и машина, сердито завывая, выбрасывая из-под колёс ошмётки грязи, начнёт медленно оседать сантиметр за сантиметром, пока не сядет на дифер.

Перед деревней Низовка разлилась широченная лужа. Страшен её вид – там и сям из воды вздыбились слеги, торчит пучками облепленный грязью хворост. Шофёры прозвали эту лужу 'Чёртов пруд'. Через неё надо ехать только по правой стороне, да и то не слишком-то надейся на удачу.

После Низовки, не доезжая соснового бора, дорога так избита, что лучше свернуть в сторону, проехать по кромке поля вновь пробитой колеёй. Зато дальше, пока не кончится сосновый бор, – песок. Дожди не размывают его, прибивают, делают плотным. Можно включить третью скорость, облегчённо откинуться на сиденье, дать газ . . . Какое наслаждение следить, как надвигаются и проносятся мимо сосны! Но только три километра душевного облегчения, несколько минут отдыха – и снова колдобины, до краёв заполненные водой, снова врытые глубоко в землю колеи, снова коварные лужи.

дифер – дифференциал

What is the narrator's attitude to the notorious, Russian country 'road', and how is this evident in his use of diction and syntax?

How does the structure of the passage contribute to its impact? After having completed your appreciation, do you consider Tendryakov a distinctive stylist, sensitively employing the resources of the Russian language?

М. И. АЛИГЕ́Р

В мире, где живёт глухой художник,
дождик не шумит,
                                  не лает пёс.
Полон мир внезапностей тревожных,
неожиданных немых угроз.

А вокруг слепого пианиста
в яркий полдень не цветут цветы:
мир звучит встревоженно и чисто
из незримой плотной пустоты.

Лишь во сне глухому вдруг приснится
шум дождя и звонкий лай собак.
А слепому – летняя криница,
полдень,
                    одуванчик или мак.

... Всё мне снится, снится сила духа,
странный и раскованный талант.
Кто же я, художник ли без слуха
или же незрячий музыкант?

(1970)

криница – ручей

What is the theme of this apparently simple poem, and how is
it developed?
Consider Aliger's diction and its effectiveness. Is there variety
in her use of metre and rhythmical form, and what does it
contribute to the poem as a whole? Consider her use of
synaesthesia.
Do you consider that she succeeds in giving her ideas 'a local
habitation and a name'?

А. П. ЧЁХОВ –
Ионыч

(1898)

Когда в губернском городе С. приезжие жаловались на скуку и однообразие жизни, то местные жители, как бы оправдываясь, говорили, что, напротив, в С. очень хорошо, что в С. есть библиотека, театр, клуб, бывают балы, что, наконец, есть умные, интересные, приятные семьи, с которыми можно завести знакомства. И указывали на семью Туркиных, как на самую образованную и талантливую.

Эта семья жила на главной улице, возле губернатора, в собственном доме. Сам Туркин, Иван Петрович, полный, красивый брюнет с бакенами, устраивал любительские спектакли с благотворительною целью, сам играл старых генералов и при этом кашлял очень смешно. Он знал много анекдотов, шарад, поговорок, любил шутить и острить, и всегда у него было такое выражение, что нельзя было понять, шутит ли он или говорит серьёзно. Жена его, Вера Иосифовна, худощавая, миловидная дама в *pince-nez*, писала повести и романы и охотно читала их вслух своим гостям. Дочь, Екатерина Ивановна, молодая девушка, играла на рояле. Одним словом, у каждого члена семьи был какой-нибудь свой талант. Туркины принимали гостей радушно и показывали им свои таланты весело, с сердечной простотой. В большом каменном доме было просторно и летом прохладно, половина окон выходила в старый тенистый сад, где весной пели соловьи; когда в доме сидели гости, то в кухне стучали ножами, во дворе пахло жареным луком – и это всякий раз предвещало обильный и вкусный ужин.

What is the narrator's attitude to the town of S. and the Turkin family, and how does he show it?
Does the structure of the passage contribute to the tone in any way?
How would you characterise Chekhov's style in terms of

vocabulary, rhythm, phraseology, syntax and imagery?
Of him Tolstoy said: 'Chekhov, like the Impressionists, has a style all his own', while Gor′ky says: 'After Chekhov it is impossible to write carelessly'. What do you think they meant, and why?

Н. С. ТИ́ХОНОВ –
Пушка
(1920)

Как мокрые раздавленные сливы,
У лошадей раскосые глаза,
Лоскутья умирающей крапивы
На колесе, сползающем назад.

Трясётся холм от ужаса, как карлик,
Услышавший циклопью болтовню,
И скоро облачной нехватит марли
На перевязки раненому дню.

Циклопом правит мальчик с канарейку,
Он веселей горящего куста,
Ударную за хвост он ловит змейку, –
Поймает, и циклоп загрохотал.

И оба так дружны и так согласны,
Что, кончив быть горластым палачом,
Когда его циклопий глаз погаснет, –
Он мальчика сажает на плечо.

И лошади их тащат по откосу –
Бездельников – двумя рядами пар,
И мальчик свёртывает папиросу,
Кривую, как бегущая тропа.

ударная змейка – gun cord

What significant uses of diction signal the poem's tone?
Which of the following formal elements do you consider
striking and/or effective, and why: vocabulary, phraseology,
imagery, rhythm and metrical form, sound pattern?

В. А. СОЛОУ́ХИН –
Мать-мачеха
(1964)

Ну и, конечно, главное украшение чёрной ещё, неприглядной ещё апрельской земли – песня жаворонка. Рыженький комочек вспархивал шагах в двадцати от дороги, расправлял трепещущие крылышки и вдруг на некоторой высоте рассыпался, брызгнув во все стороны, на пригоршни золотых, серебряных, малиновых звуков.

Песенка поднималась всё выше в голубизну, до того, что сам трепещущий колокольчик сливался с голубизной. Но чем выше поднималась песенка, тем слаще, тем радостнее казалась она, тем больше ликования рождалось навстречу ей в душе очарованного человека. И ведь настолько она щедра, что не нужно бояться, будто уйдёшь и ничего не будет. Прошёл сто шагов, километр, а песенка по-прежнему над твоей головой. Она идёт вслед, непременная, как точка зенита. Куда бы ни ушёл, всегда над головой зенит. Воображение охватывает сначала зримую глазом округу, потом на двести, на триста вёрст вдаль и вширь. Над всей землёй, над всей вселенной Россией, куда бы ты ни пошёл или где бы ни оказался чудом, – всюду сейчас одновременно (одновременно ведь, чёрт возьми!) звенит золотая жавороночья песня. Сколько же золотых колокольчиков подвешено сейчас в голубизне над всей-то землёй? Это сама земля поёт, само небо поёт, само солнце поёт. Это их вечная весенняя песня. И что этой песне до тебя, забаррикадировавшегося в прокуренной аудитории? Песня жила, когда тебя не было и в помине, когда не было не только прокуренной аудитории, но и каменного дома того, и каменного города того. И если пройдут века и снова вдруг не будет никакого города, золотые колокольчики всё равно затрепещут над землёй в урочное апрельское время.

How is the theme of the extract developed, and what is the overall·pattern of the sentence relationships?

Comment on the dominant images in the passage, and its type of vocabulary and phraseology.
What role do sentence rhythm and syntax play in the apotheosis of such a minute subject?

Н. А. КЛЮЕВ –
Старуха
(1912)

Сын обижает, невестка не слухает,
Хлебным куском да бездельем корит,
Чую – на кладбище колокол ухает,
Ладаном тянет от вешних ракит.

Вышла я в поле, седая, горбатая, –
Нива без прясла, кругом сирота . . .
Свесила верба серёжки мохнатые,
Мёда душистей, белее холста.

Верба-невеста, молодка пригожая,
Зеленью-платом не засти зари!
Аль с алоцветной красою не схожа я –
Косы желтее, чем бус янтари.

Аль сарафан с расписной оторочкою,
Белый рукав и плясун-башмачок . . .
Хворым младенчиком, всхлипнув над кочкою,
Звон оголосил пролесок и лог.

Схожа я мшистой, заплаканной ивою,
Мне ли крутиться в янтарь-бахрому . . .
Зой-невидимка узывней, дремливее,
Белые вербы в кадильном дыму.

прясло – решётка из жердей на столбах для сушки снопов
пролесок – перелесок   зой – жужжанье насекомых
узывный – зазывной   чую – слышу

Is this simply a poem about an old peasant woman?
What aspects of the style of the poem render it an appropriate
vehicle for its theme?

А. Н. ОСТРО́ВСКИЙ –
Гроза
(1859)

КАТЕРИНА (*одна, держа ключ в руках*): Что она это делает-то? Что она только придумывает? Ах, сумасшедшая, право сумасшедшая! Вот погибель-то! Вот она! Бросить его, бросить далеко, в реку кинуть, чтоб не нашли никогда. Он руки-то жжёт, точно уголь. (*Подумав*) Вот так-то и гибнет наша сестра-то. В неволе-то кому весело! Мало ли что в голову-то придёт. Вышел случай, другая и рада: так, очертя голову, и кинется. А как же это можно, не подумавши, не рассудивши-то! Долго ли в беду попасть! А там и плачься всю жизнь, мучайся; неволя-то ещё горчее покажется. (*Молчание*) А горька неволя, ох, как горька! Кто от неё не плачет! А пуще всех мы, бабы. Вот хоть я теперь? Живу, маюсь, просвету не вижу! Да и не увижу, знать! Что дальше, то хуже. А теперь ещё этот грех-то на меня. (*Задумывается*) Кабы не свекровь! ... Сокрушила она меня ... от неё мне и дом-то опостылел; стены-то даже противны. (*Задумчиво смотрит на ключ*) Бросить его? Разумеется, надо бросить. И как он это ко мне в руки попал? На соблазн, на пагубу мою. (*Прислушивается*) Ах, кто-то идёт. Так сердце и упало. (*Прячет ключ в карман*) Нет! ... Никого ... Что я так испугалась! И ключ спрятала. Ну, уж знать там ему и быть! Видно, сама судьба того хочет! Да какой же в этом грех, если я взгляну на него раз, хоть издали-то! Да хоть и поговорю-то, так всё не беда! А как же я мужу-то! ... Да ведь он сам не захотел. Да может, такого и случая-то ещё во всю жизнь не выйдет. Тогда и плачься на себя: был случай, да не умела пользоваться. Да что я говорю-то, что я себя обманываю? Мне хоть умереть, да увидеть его. Перед кем я притворяюсь-то! ... Бросить ключ! Нет, ни за что на свете! Он мой теперь ... Будь что будет, а я Бориса увижу! Ах, кабы ночь поскорее! ...

она – her sister-in law, Varvara, who has just given her the key.
наша сестра-то – we women.
вот хоть я теперь – what's *my* life like, for instance?

173

свекровь – her tyrannically traditional mother-in-law, Kabanova.
ну, уж знать там ему и быть! – well, it really looks like that's where it's meant to be!
Бориса – Boris Kuligin, her secret lover.

Katerina, the highly sensitive, oppressed heroine of Ostrovsky's naturalistic drama of the spiritual desolation of life among the mid-nineteenth-century merchant-classes, has just been given the opportunity, in the form of a key, to escape virtual confinement to see her lover. This passage dramatises her confused responses. N.B. the extensive and often untranslatable use of particles to convey the flavour of the contemporary speech of her social stratum.

Trace the development of Katerina's changing responses and show how Ostrovsky conveys them in his use of language, syntax and punctuation. To what extent do stage directions contribute to this development?

Н. С. ГУМИЛЁВ –
Слово
(1921)

В оный день, когда над миром новым
Бог склонял лицо Своё, тогда
Солнце останавливали словом,
Словом разрушали города.

И орёл не взмахивал крылами,
Звёзды жались в ужасе к луне,
Если, точно розовое пламя,
Слово проплывало в вышине.

А для низкой жизни были числа,
Как домашний, подъяремный скот,
Потому, что все оттенки смысла
Умное число передаёт.

Патриарх седой, себе под руку
Покоривший и добро и зло,
Не решаясь обратиться к звуку,
Тростью на песке чертил число.

Но забыли мы, что осиянно
Только слово средь земных тревог,
И в Евангельи от Иоанна
Сказано, что слово это Бог.

Мы ему поставили пределом
Скудные пределы естества,
И, как пчёлы в улье опустелом,
Дурно пахнут мёртвые слова.

крылами – крыльями   осиянно – ярко освещено

How do imagery, diction, rhythm and metre contribute to the
poetic expression of this highly abstract theme?

А. М. РЁМИЗОВ –

Подстриженными глазами

(1951)

И разве могу забыть я блистающее утро – блестящее, такое тёплое, как только летом, а только что наступил май, и сквозь сон всю залитую солнцем нашу тесную детскую, когда меня разбудили, но меня разбудил не колокол Андроньева монастыря, свободно, легко и властно катящийся тяжёлым чугуном поверх зелёных огородов и всегда с какою-то серебряною нежностью касающийся моего слуха, меня разбудил торжественный необычайный шум – и этот шум, мне показалось, был от крыльев огромных птиц, кружащихся над самой крышей, и, может, таких же, как солнце, жарких, и вот отчего тепло так – и вдруг прикосновением холодных пальцев насторожила меня: или оттого, что в этом торжественном шуме и шарыгающих крыльях я почуял затаившееся внимание, а в комнате никого не было. Я вскочил с кровати и опрометью бросился в соседнюю комнату, откуда из окон видно – через сад – торчали две огромные кирпичные трубы с иглой громоотвода и рядом красный досиня сверкающими окнами фабричный корпус – сахарный завод Вогау: И я увидел у раскрытых окон и няньку, и её дочь, приехавшую вчера из Зарайской деревни и ночевавшую с нами, и всех моих братьев. И когда за всеми потянулся я посмотреть, меня обдало жаром: горел сахарный завод. Синее, тающее, крутящееся колесом пламя и сквозь расплавленную синь из синющего сердца густая каплями кровь, и эта огненная синь дышала жаром, и не птицы, слепые крылатые звери – распущенная, разодранная шкура, – тяжело вылезали, продираясь из кипящих металлических масс и, шарыгая крыльями, душно лезли через сад к окну. И вдруг жгучая мысль, как расплавленная капля, с болью пронзила меня, я понял что-то – вспомнил, как вспоминается давно когда-то бывшее скрытое, вдруг вспыхивающее пожаром, и, горя, я поднял руки к огню, – пламень взвивался надо мной, и пламень вырезался из сердца – пламя окружало меня . . .

шарыгать – медленно взмахивать

What is the author's attitude to the highly memorable events described, and to what extent does it dictate his choice of language, use of syntax and the overall structure?

Comment in detail on Remizov's language and phraseology in this passage.

What are the contributions of rhythm and sound pattern to the effect of this passage?

Э. Г. БАГРИ́ЦКИЙ –
Осень
(1915)

Литавры лебедей замолкли вдалеке,
Затихли журавли за топкими лугами,
Лишь ястреба кружат над рыжими стогами,
Да осень шелестит в прибрежном тростнике.

На сломанных плетнях завился гибкий хмель,
И никнет яблоня, и утром пахнет слива,
В весёлых кабачках разлито в бочки пиво,
И в тихой мгле полей, дрожа, звучит свирель.

Над прудом облака – жемчужны и легки,
На западе огни – прозрачны и лиловы.
Запрятавшись в кусты, мальчишки-птицеловы
В тени зелёных хвой расставили силки.

Из золотых полей, где синий дым встаёт,
Проходят девушки за грузными возами,
Их бёдра зыблются под тонкими холстами,
На их щеках – загар, как золотистый мёд.

В осенние луга, в безудержный простор
Спешат охотники под кружевом тумана,
И в зыбкой сырости пронзительно и странно
Звучит дрожащий лай нашедших зверя свор.

И осень пьяная бредёт из тёмных чащ,
Натянут тёмный лук холодными руками,
И в лето целится и пляшет под лугами,
На смуглое плечо накинув жёлтый плащ.

И поздняя заря на алтарях лесов
Сжигает тёмный нард и брызжет алой кровью,
И к дёрну летнему, и сырому изголовью,
Летит холодный шум спадающих плодов.

What formal devices serve to make this poem an impersonal
and static vision of Autumn?

В. П. КАТА́ЕВ –
Время, вперёд!

(1932)

Будильник затарахтел, как жестянка с монпансье. Будильник был дешёвый, крашеный, коричневый, советского производства.

Половина седьмого.

Часы шли верно. Но Маргулиес не спал. Он встал в шесть и опередил время. Ещё не было случая, чтобы будильник действительно поднял его. Маргулиес не мог доверять такому, в сущности, простому механизму, как часы, такую драгоценную вещь, как время.

Триста шесть разделить на восемь. Затем шестьдесят разделить на тридцать восемь и две десятых.

Это Маргулиес сосчитал в уме мгновенно.

Получается – один и приблизительно пять десятых.

Числа имели следующее значение:

Триста шесть – количество замесов. Восемь – количество рабочих часов. Шестьдесят – количество минут в часе.

Таким образом, харьковские бетонщики делали один замес в одну и приблизительно пять десятых минуты, то есть в девяносто секунд. Из этих девяноста секунд вычесть шестьдесят секунд обязательно минимума, необходимо по каталогу на замес. Оставалось тридцать секунд.

Тридцать секунд на подвоз материалов, на загрузку и подъём ковша. Теоретически возможно. Но практически? Вопрос. Надо разобраться.

До сих пор на строительстве лучшие бригады бетонщиков делали не больше двухсот замесов в смену. Это считалось прекрасной нормой. Теперь положение резко менялось.

Лезвием безопасной бритвы Маргулиес очинил жёлтый карандаш. Он очинил его со щегольством и небрежной ловкостью молодого инженера, снимая длинные, виртуозно тонкие полированные стружки.

На горе рвали руду. Стучали частые, беспорядочные взрывы. Воздух ломался мягко, как грифельная доска.

Маргулиес – an engineer and one of the main characters in this 'production novel' which deals with an attempt by a brigade at Magnitogorsk to break the world concrete-mixing record.

харьковские бетонщики – the record-holders of Khar'kov in the Ukraine.

Despite its ostensibly intractable subject-matter what makes this passage readable? Comment in your answer on significant use of syntax, diction and imagery.

Г. Р. ДЕРЖА́ВИН –
Павлин

(1795)

Какое гордое творенье,
Хвост пышно расширяя свой,
Черно-зелёны в искрах перья
С рассыпною бахромой
Позадь чешуйной груди кажет,
Как некий круглый, дивный свет?

Лазурно-сизы-бирюзовы
На каждого конце пера,
Тенисты круги, волны новы
Струиста злата и сребра;
Наклонит – изумруды блещут!
Повернет – яхонты горят!

Не то ли славный царь пернатый?
Не то ли райска птица Жар,
Которой столь убор богатый
Приводит в удивленье тварь?
Где ступит – радуги играют!
Где станет – там лучи вокруг!

Конечно, сила и паренье
Орлиные в её крылах,
Глас трубный, лебедино пенье
В её пресладостных устах;
А пеликана добродетель
В её и сердце и душе!

Но что за чудное явленье?
Я слышу некий странный визг!
Сей феникс опустил вдруг перья,
Увидя гнусность ног своих.
О пышность! как ты ослепляешь!
И барин без ума – павлин.

птица Жар – the Fire-bird of Russian folk-lore with brilliant shining feathers.

пеликана добродетель – the pelican, according to Egyptian legend, is such a noble bird that, by swallowing snakes, it frees the Earth from their poison, and so compassionate that it feeds its young with the blood from its own breast.

феникс – according to Egyptian mythology the Phoenix was a beautiful bird which lived for 500 years. At the end of this period it is consumed by flames, but rises again from the ashes.

What aspects of this poem place it firmly in the eighteenth-century poetic tradition?

After studying it carefully, what do you consider are the poem's strengths and weaknesses?

В. В. РО́ЗАНОВ –

В мире неясного и нерешённого

(1899)

Мы уже заметили, что *теперь* опочивальня супругов во многих благочестных семьях преобразуется (как и указано Апостолом) в 'домашнюю церковь'. Она чиста, уединённа, с образом, горящею лампадою. Важная вещь в супружестве – *чистота тела*; вот отчего 'путь спасения в браке' требует обязательных вечерних омовений, или всего тела, или лица, кистей рук, ступеней ног, и особенно персей и всей области corpus'а от колен до пояса (где проходит 'жила, тронутая Богом у Иакова во время борьбы с ним ночью'). Дабы освободить их от пыли (физики) и всей суеты дня (психики). Припомнив первую строку 'Песни песней': 'да лобзает он меня лобзанием уст своих' – все обнажаемые части должны быть чисты, как мы обычно держим чисто уста. Но вот ещё мысль. Образ, конечно, должен сопровождать нас всюду. У русских так и есть. 'Без Бога ни до порога'. Но странно, и к большому нравственному стыду, что одно, и притом излюбленное древней Русью место – *баня*, всегда и только одно бывает лишено его. И, между тем, это единственное место, где человек бывает без одежд, как сотворил его, *ещё до греха*, Бог. Между тем образ и особенно мерцающие лучи лампады льющиеся кругом, наполняющие небольшое это помещение, обливая всю полноту тела, рождали бы таинственным своим действием невинность те́ла. Известно теперь целебное физическое действие солнечных и электрических лучей. Вообще кожа человека глубоко *духовна*; она эстетична, – а эстетика есть дух; и где возможна эстетика, непре́менно возможна и нравственность. Вот достижение *кожной* нравственности, наконец, и *кожной невинности, кожного целомудрия, кожной святости* – должны составить одну из великих проблем в браке. И мерцающий свет лампады, *свет религиозный*, смешиваясь физически с обливаемым им corpus'ом отражающим этот падающий на него свет, – в десятилетиях, в веках, мог бы повести к священному исцелению тела нашего 'от греха, проклятия и смерти'.

Rozanov is considered one of the most original and idiosyncratic stylists in Russian literature. Attempt an appreciation of this, not impenetrable, extract without guidance.

Н. КОРЖА́ВИН –
Дети в Освенциме
(1961)

Мужчины мучали детей.
Умно. Намеренно. Умело.
Творили будничное дело,
Трудились – мучали детей.

И это каждый раз опять, –
Кляня, ругаясь без причины ...
И детям было не понять,
Чего хотят от них мужчины.

За что – обидные слова,
Побои, голод, псов рычанье?
И дети думали сперва,
Что это за непослушанье.

Они представить не могли
Того, что было всем открыто:
По древней логике земли,
От взрослых дети ждут защиты.

А дни все шли, как смерть страшны,
И дети стали образцовы,
Но их всё били.
                    Так же.
                              Снова.
И не снимали с них вины.

Они хватались за людей.
Они молили. И любили.
Но у мужчин 'идеи' были,
Мужчины мучали детей.

Я жив. Дышу. Люблю людей.
Но жизнь бывает мне постыла,
Как только вспомню: это –было.
Мужчины мучали детей.

Освенцим – Auschwitz

Considering tone, structure, diction and rhythm, what gives this poem its shocking impact?

В. Ф. ПАНО́ВА –
Спутники
(1946)

Его мобилизовали сразу.

Это был страшный день. В первый раз она увидела, что в его жизни первое место занимает не она.

Он двигался по комнате, собирая какие-то свои вещи, и рассеянно отвечал ей . . .

Она не обиделась. Дело было не в обиде. Просто впервые она увидела его с этой стороны.

Первое место в его жизни занимало какое-то мужское дело, сейчас это дело призывало его. Он ещё не ушёл, а уже он ей не принадлежал.

Иначе не могло быть. Она закрыла лицо руками. Если бы было иначе, она разлюбила бы его.

Нет. Не разлюбила, – разлюбить невозможно; но торжество её померкло бы. Она была спортсменка, амазонка, победительница в состязаниях, она понимала такие вещи. Торжествовать можно только победу над сильным. Много ли чести победить слабое сердце? У него было сильное сердце. Она гордилась им.

Что-то надо сделать, чтобы он понял, как она всё это поняла. Чтобы он ушёл довольный ею.

Прежде всего надо скрыть своё отчаяние. Он хорошо держится – просто, спокойно. Шутит. Она тоже может так.

И надо помочь ему собраться. Уселась, сложила руки, как в гостях. Вот он кладёт в рюкзак рубашку, а на ней нет пуговиц, она помнит.

– постой, Даня, я сама.

Она вынула бельё из рюкзака и всё пересмотрела и починила. Собрала провизию – немного, он так просил. Напомнила взять тазик и кисточку для бритья. И крем для сапог. И щётку. Уложила конверты, бумагу, спички. Он сел и смотрел, как она укладывает его вещи. И это тоже так и должно быть: муж сидит, отдыхая, и курит, пока жена снаряжает его на войну.

How does the narrator achieve the poignant tone of this passage, and how does she prevent it from degenerating into sentimentality?

What do language and syntax contribute to the effectiveness of this extract?

Б. АХМАДУЛИНА –
Газированная вода
(1960)

Вот к будке с газированной водой,
всех автоматов баловень надменный,
таинственный ребёнок современный
подходит, как к игрушке заводной.

Затем, самонадеянный фантаст,
монету влажную он опускает в щёлку,
и, нежным брызгам подставляя щёку,
стаканом ловит розовый фонтан.

О, мне б его уверенность на миг
и фамильярность с тайною простою!
Но нет, я этой милости не стою,
пускай прольётся мимо рук моих.

А мальчуган, причастный чудесам,
несёт в ладони семь стеклянных граней,
и отблеск их летит на красный гравий
и больно ударяет по глазам.

Робея, я сама вхожу в игру
и поддаюсь с блаженным чувством риска
соблазну металлического диска,
и замираю, и стакан беру.

Воспрянув из серебряных оков,
родится омут сладкий и солёный,
неведомым дыханьем населённый
и свежей толчеёю пузырьков.

Все радуги, возникшие из них,
пронзают небо в сладости короткой,
и вот уже, разнеженный щекоткой,
семь вкусов спектра пробует язык.

И автомата тёмная душа
взирает с добротою старомодной,
словно крестьянка, что рукой холодной
даст путнику напиться из ковша.

How does the poetess convey her feelings about the events
described?

How do the formal elements of the poem (e.g. structure,
rhythm and metrical form, vocabulary, phraseology, imagery,
sound pattern) serve to make the ostensibly banal magical?

А. Д. СИНЯ́ВСКИЙ-ТЕРЦ –

Пхенц

(1961)

Лет пятнадцать назад мне довелось познакомиться с учебником по анатомии. Желая быть в курсе дел, я внимательно изучил все картинки и диаграммы. Затем в Парке культуры и отдыха имени Горького я имел возможность наблюдать купающихся в реке мальчишек. Но видеть живьём раздетую женщину, да ещё на близком расстоянии, мне раньше не приходилось.

Повторяю, это – ужасно. Она вся оказалась такого же неестественно-белого цвета, как её шея, лицо и руки. Спереди болталась пара белых грудей. Я принял их вначале за вторичные руки, ампутированные выше локтя. Но каждая заканчивалась круглой присоской, похожей на кнопку звонка.

А дальше – до самых ног – всё свободное место занимал шаровидный живот. Здесь собирается в одну кучу проглоченная за день еда. Нижняя её половина, будто голова, поросла кудрявыми волосами.

Меня издавна волновала проблема пола, играющая первостепенную роль в их умственной и нравственной жизни. Должно быть, в целях безопасности она окутана с древних времён покровом непроницаемой тайны. Даже в учебнике по анатомии об этом предмете ничего не говорится или сказано туманно и вскользь, так, чтобы не догадались.

И теперь, поборов оторопь, я решил воспользоваться моментом и заглянул туда, где – как написано в учебнике – помещается детородный аппарат, выстреливающий наподобие катапульты готовых младенцев.

Там я мельком увидел что-то похожее на лицо человека. Только это, как мне показалось, было не женское, а мужское лицо, пожилое, небритое, с оскаленными зубами.

Голодный злой мужчина обитал у неё между ног. Вероятно, он храпел по ночам и сквернословил от скуки. Должно быть отсюда происходит двуличие женской натуры, про которое метко сказал поэт Лермонтов: 'прекрасна, как ангел небесный, как демон коварна и зла'.

мне – an alien vegetable creature called Pkhents, which has taken human form.
в Парке . . . – Gor′ky Park, a large recreation area on the left bank of the Moscow River.

Find out the meaning of *остранение* as a term in literary criticism and show how it determines tone, structure and use of language in this extract.

Л. Н. МАРТЫ́НОВ –
Мороз
(1946)

Мороз был – сорок! Город был как ночью.
Из недр метро, как будто из вулканов,
Людских дыханий вырывались клочья
И исчезали, ввысь бесследно канув.

И всё ж на стужу было непохоже:
Никто ничто не проклинал сквозь губы,
Ни у кого озноб не шёл по коже.
Сквозь снежный блеск, бушуя, плыли шубы.

Куда? Конечно, в звонкое от зноя,
Давно уже родившееся где-то
Пшеничное, ржаное и льняное,
Как белый хлопок, взрывчатое лето.

Казалось, это видят даже дети:
С серпом, силком и рыболовной сетью
То лето, величайшее на свете,
В цветы одето посреди столетья!

То лето – как великая победа,
И суховеи отошли в преданья,
И пьют росу из тракторного следа
Какие-то крылатые созданья.

И неохота ни большим, ни малым
Пренебрегать цветами полевыми,
И зной дневной скреплён закатом алым
С теплейшими ночами грозовыми.

Ведь нет сильнее этого желанья,
Мечта такая – сколько красоты в ней,
Что зимние студёные дыханья
Вернутся в мир в обличье чистых ливней!

Вот что хотелось увидать воочью,
И было надо настоять на этом.
Мороз был – сорок! Город был как ночью,
Как ночью перед ветреным рассветом.

Having completed your appreciation of this poem, do you
consider that Martynov deserves to be more widely known? If
so, for what artistic reasons?

В. П. НЕКРА́СОВ –

Кира Георгиевна

(1961)

Жизнь у Киры Георгиевны – или, как её называли друзья, Кили (в детстве она долго не могла произнести букву 'р') – поначалу сложилась как будто весело и легко. Родилась и жила она до войны в Киеве. Отец был врачом-отоларингологом – слово, которое Киля тоже очень долго не могла выговорить, мать, как пишут в анкетах, домохозяйкой. Был ещё младший брат Мишка – лентяй, футболист и первый во дворе драчун.

Учась в школе, Киля мечтала стать балериной и ходила даже в балетную студию, потом, поступив в скучнейшую ненавистную ей торгово-промышленную профшколу ('почему-то надо обязательно куда-то поступать'), стала мечтать о карьере киноактрисы – она была стройненькой, с весёлыми глазами, кудрявой, подстриженной под мальчика, и профшкольные друзья уверяли её, что она исключительно фотогенична (в то время очень модным было это слово). В зеркале на её туалете появились фотографии знаменитых киноартистов тех лет. Одно время она носила даже чёлочку а-ля Лиа де-Путти. Потом она остыла к кино и увлекалась живописью, очень левой, приводившей её добропорядочных родителей в ужас. На экзамене в художественный институт старика швейцара, позировавшего экзаменующимся, сделала зелёным и под Сезанна. Тем не менее её приняли – правда, не на живописный, а почему-то на скульптурный факультет.

В институте было весело и не очень утомительно. Приятно было ходить с этюдником, отмывать бензином на платье масляную краску и глину, с профессиональным апломбом рассуждать о колорите, густоте тона, прозрачности теней, восторгаться Матиссом, Гогеном, Майолем, скептически улыбаться, когда упоминали Сурикова или Антокольского. В институте она научилась курить. Там же она влюбилась. Сперва в Сашку Лозинского, своего однокурсника, физкультурника, певца и гитариста, потом в очкастого Ваньку Лифшица, писавшего стихи. Ванька ввёл её в кружок поэтов. Там оказалось ещё веселее. Читали друг другу стихи, свои и чужие, писали пародии, спорили, острили, бродили ночами по надднепровским паркам, немножко пили – не столько по охоте, сколько для взрелости. Там же она познакомилась с Вадимом Кудрявцевым.

Лиа де-Путти – Lya de Putti, born Budapest 1901, died New York 1931, starred in numerous German, British and American films of the twenties. She was memorable more for her decorative appearance than for her acting ability.

под Сезанна – Paul Cézanne (1839–1906), influential, French post-Impressionist painter (and precursor of Cubism).

Матиссом, Гогеном, Майолем – Henri Matisse (1869–1954), French painter, leader of the 'Fauve' movement, who emphasised form, design and colour at the expense of verisimilitude and thus made an important step towards abstract art. Paul Gauguin (1848–1903), French post-Impressionist painter, and forerunner of expressionist tendencies in twentieth-century art. Aristide Maillol (1861–1944), a French 'synthetist' sculptor.

Сурикова или Антокольского – V. I. Surikov (1848–1916), Russian historical and genre painter, and member of the Peredvizhniki, a group of painters who formed an association in the late nineteenth century with the object of sending travelling exhibitions to the provinces. M. M. Antokol'sky (1843–1902), a Russian realist sculptor.

What is the underlying theme of this extract and how does its tone suggest Nekrasov's purpose? What significant uses of diction and syntax reveal this tone?

How does the passage's structure contribute to the impact of the last sentence?

How might you describe Nekrasov's vocabulary and phraseology?

To what extent is his style reminiscent of Chekhov's (q.v.)? Include a reference to prose rhythm in your answer.

И. БРÓДСКИЙ

Был чёрный небосвод светлей тех ног,
И слиться с темнотою он не мог.
В тот вечер возле нашего огня
Увидели мы чёрного коня.

Не помню я чернее ничего.
Как уголь, были ноги у него.
Он чёрен был, как ночь, как пустота.
Он чёрен был от гривы до хвоста.
Но чёрной по-другому уж была
Спина его, не знавшая седла.
Недвижно он стоял. Казалось, спит.
Пугала чернота его копыт.

Он чёрен был, не чувствовал теней.
Так чёрен, что не делался темней.
Так чёрен, как полуночная мгла.
Так чёрен, как внутри себя игла.
Так чёрен, как деревья впереди.
Как место между рёбрами и в груди.
Как ямка под землёю, где зерно.
Я думаю: внутри у нас черно.

Но всё-таки чернел он на глазах!
Была всего лишь полночь на часах.
Он к нам не приближался ни на шаг.
В паху его царил бездонный мрак.
Спина его была уж не видна.
Не оставалось светлого пятна.
Глаза его белели, как щелчок.
Ещё страшнее был его зрачок.

Как будто он был чей-то негатив.
Зачем же он, свой бег остановив,
Меж нами оставался до утра?
Зачем не отходил он от костра?
Зачем он чёрным воздухом дышал,
Раздавленными сучьями шуршал?
Зачем струил он чёрный свет из глаз?

Он всадника искал себе средь нас.

(1961)

Consider in detail how the author succeeds in galvanising a relatively unoriginal theme.

В. М. ГА́РШИН –
Красный цветок
(1883)

Он сознавал, что он в сумасшедшем доме; он сознавал даже, что он болен. Иногда, как в первую ночь, он про́сыпался среди тишины после целого дня буйного движения, чувствуя ломоту во всех членах и страшную тяжесть в голове, но в полном сознании. Может быть, отсутствие впечатлений в ночной тишине и полусвете, может быть, слабая работа мозга только что проснувшегося человека делали то, что в такие минуты он ясно понимал своё положение и был как будто бы здоров. Но наступал день; вместе со светом и пробуждением жизни в больнице его снова волною охватывали впечатления; больной мозг не мог справиться с ними, и он снова был безумным. Его состояние было странною смесью правильных суждений и нелепостей. Он понимал, что вокруг него все больные, но в то же время в каждом из них какое-нибудь тайно скрывающееся или скрытое лицо, которое он знал прежде или о котором читал или слыхал. Больница́ была населена людьми всех времён и всех стран. Тут были и живые и мёртвые. Тут были знаменитые и сильные мира и солдаты, убитые в последнюю войну и воскресшие. Он видел себя в каком-то волшебном, заколдованном круге, собравшем в себя всю силу земли, и в горделивом исступлении считал себя за центр этого круга. Все они, его товарищи по больнице, собрались сюда затем, чтобы исполнить дело, смутно представлявшееся ему гигантским предприятием, направленным к уничтожению зла на земле. Он не знал, в чём оно будет состоять, но чувствовал в себе достаточно сцлы для его исполнения. Он мог читать мысли других людей; видел в вещах всю их историю; большие вязы в больничном саду рассказывали ему целые легенды из пережитого; здание, действительно построенное довольно давно, он считал постройкой Петра Великого и был уверен, что царь жил в нём в эпоху Полтавской битвы. Он прочёл это на стенах, на обвалившейся штукатурке, на кусках кирпича и изразцов, находимых им в саду; вся история дома и сада была написана на них. Он населил маленькое здание мертвецкой десятками и сотнями давно умерших людей и пристально вглядывался в оконце, выходившее из её подвала в уголок сада, видя в неровном отражении света в старом радужном и грязном стекле знакомые черты, виденные им когда-то в жизни или на портретах.

Петра Великого – Peter I (the Great) (1683–1721), the great and tyrannical Westerniser of Russian life who defeated the Swedes at the battle of Poltava in 1709.

How does the narrator develop and make consistent the inmate's delusions?

What is the narrator's attitude to his subject-matter and what are the linguistic/syntactic pointers to this attitude?

Having studied vocabulary, syntax and sentence rhythms, how would you characterise Garshin's style?

В. Я. БРЮСОВ –
Замкнутые
(1901)

Весь Город был овеян тайной лет.
Он был угрюм и дряхл, но горд и строен.
На узких улицах дрожал ослабший свет,
И каждый резкий звук казался там устроен.
В проходах тёмных, полных тишины,
Неслышно прятались пристанища торговли;
Углами острыми нарушив ход стены,
Кончали дом краснеющие кровли;
Виднелись с улицы в готическую дверь
Огромные и сумрачные сени,
Где вечно нежились сырые тени . . .
И затворялся вход, ворча, как зверь.

Из серых камней выведены строго,
Являли церкви мощь свободных сил.
В них дух столетий смело воплотил
И веру и гений свой, и веру в Бога.
Передавался труд к потомкам от отца,
Но каждый камень, взвешен и размерен,
Ложился в свой черёд по замыслу творца,
И линий общий строй был строг и верен,
И каждый малый свод продуман до конца
В стремленьи ввысь, величественно смелом.
Вершилось здание свободным остриём,
И было конченным, и было целым,
Спокойно замкнутым в себе самом.

В музеях запертых, в торжественном покое,
Хранились бережно останки старины –
Одежды, утвари, оружие былое,
Трофеи победительной войны:
То кормы лодок дерзких мореходов,

То кубки с обликом суровых лиц,
Знамёна покорявшихся народов
Да клювы неизвестных птиц.
И всё в себе былую жизнь таило,
Иных столетий пламенную дрожь.
Как в ветер верило истлевшее ветрило!
Как жаждал мощных рук ещё сверкавший нож!...
И всё кругом пустынно-глухо было.

Having studied this extract in detail, what do you think Bely meant by his often-quoted description of Bryusov as 'поэт мрамора и бронза'? (Consider especially the frequency and prominence of nouns, adjectives and verbs, phraseology, rhythm and metrical form, sound pattern.)

Н. С. ЛЕСКОВ –
Соборяне
(1872)

С этим он снова встал и, отойдя от опушки, увидел, что с востока, действительно, шла тёмная туча. Гроза застигала Савелия одним-одинёшенка, среди леса и полей, приготовлявшихся встретить её нестерпимое дыхание. Опять удар, нива заколебалась сильней и по ней полоснуло свежим холодом.

К чёрной туче, которою заслонён весь восток, снизу взмывали клубами меньшие тучки. Их будто что-то подтягивало и подбирало как кулисы, и по всему этому нет-нет и прорежет огнём. Точно маг, готовый дать страшное представление, в последний раз осматривает с фонарём в руке тёмную сцену, прежде чем зажжёт все огни и поднимет завесу. Чёрная туча ползёт, и чем она ближе, тем кажется непроглядней. Не пронесёт ли её Бог? Не разразится ли она где подальше? Но нет: вон, по её верхнему краю, тихо сверкнула огнистая нить и молнии замигали и зареяли разом по всей тёмной массе. Солнца уже нет: тучи покрыли его диск и его длинные, как шпаги, лучи, посветив мгновение, тоже сверкнули и скрылись. Вихорь засвистал и зещелкал. Облака заволновались точно знамёна. По бурому полю зреющей ржи запестрели широкие белые пятна и пошли ходенём; в одном месте падёт будто с неба одно, в другом – сядет широко другое и разом пойдут навстречу друг-другу, сольются и оба исчезнут. У межи при дороге ветер треплет колос так странно, что это как будто и не ветер, а кто-то живой притаился у корня и злится. По лесу шум. Вот и над лесом зигзаг; и ещё вот черкнуло совсем по верхушкам и вдруг тихо . . . всё тихо! . . . ни молний, ни ветру: всё стихло. Это тишина пред бурей: всё запоздавшее спрятать себя от невзгоды пользуется этой последнею минутой затишья; несколько пчёл пронесло мимо Туберозова, как будто они не летели, а несло их напором ветра. Из тёмной чащи кустов, которые казались теперь совсем чёрными, выскочило несколько перепуганных зайцев и залегли в меже вровень с землёю. По траве, которая при теперешнем освещениц тоже черна, как асфальт, прокатился серебристый клубок и юркнул под землю. Это ёж. Всё убралось, что куда может. Вот и последний, недавно реявший, ворон плотно сжал у плеч крылья и, ринувшись вниз, тяжело закопошился в вершине высокого дуба.

ходенём – ходуном

The subject-matter is self-evident, but how is it developed and what does this development contribute to the impact of the storm?

In your appreciation of this passage comment on its dominant images and type of vocabulary, noting the frequency, prominence and contribution of the parts of speech.

В. В. ХЛЕ́БНИКОВ –
Журавль
(1910)

И точно: трубы подымали свои шеи,
Как на стене тень пальцев ворожеи.
Так делаются подвижными дотоле
                    неподвижные на болоте выпи,
Когда опасность миновала.
Среди камышей и озёрной кипи
Птица-растение главою закивала.

Ну что же? Скачет вдоль реки в каком-то вихре
Железный, кисти руки подобный, крюк.
Стоя над волнами, когда они стихли,
Он походил на подарок на память костяку рук!
Часть к части, он стремится к вещам
                    с невидимой ещё силой,
Так узник на свидание стремится навстречу милой!
Железные и хитроумные чертоги в каком-то
                                яростном пожаре,
Как пламень, возникающий из жара,
На место становясь, давали чуду ноги.

Трубы, стоявшие века,
Летят,
Движениям подражая червяка,
Игривей в шалости котят.
Тогда части поездов, с надписью:
            'Для некурящих' и 'Для служилых',
Остов одели в сплетённые друг с другом жилы.
Железные пути срываются с дорог
Движением созревших осенью стручков.
И вот, и вот плывёт по волнам, как порог,
Как Неясыть иль грозный Детинец, от берегов
                                отпавшийся Тучков!

О род людской! Ты был как мякоть,
В которой созрели иные семена!
Чертя подошвой грозной слякоть,
Плывут восстанием на тя иные племена!
Из желез
И меди над городом восстал, грозя, костяк,
Перед которым человечество и всё иное лишь пустяк,
Не более одной желез.
Прямо летящие, в изгибе ль,
Трубы возвещают человечеству погибель.

Неясыть . . . Детинец – rapids on the river Dnieper
Тучков – The Tuchkov bridge in Petersburg, spanning the Malaya Neva and joining Vasil'evsky Island to the Peterburgskaya Storona (now Kirovskiye Ostrova).
тя – тебя (Old Church Slavonic form)

Khlebnikov, like many twentieth-century writers, feared the effects of unbridled technology on human life. What dominant symbol does he use in this excerpt from a long poem to represent this threat, and in what way(s) is it appropriate?
Is Khlebnikov's attitude to his material entirely one of alarm?
What is the structure of this excerpt?
Khlebnikov was influenced by Whitman – is it evident here and to what extent is the influence effective?
The verse-form here is not entirely free because a traditional device is used in a then novel manner – comment on this and its effectiveness.
Discuss the extract's dominant images and why they might be in ironic contrast to *журавль* and *выпь*?
Consider the range and type of vocabulary used, and phraseology. To what extent could it be called striking or original?

В. С. ГРÓССМАН –
Всё течёт

(1963)

Вот что поняла. Вначале голод из дому гонит. В первое время он, как огонь, печёт, терзает, и за кишки, и за душу рвёт – человек и бежит из дому. Люди червей копают, траву собирают, видишь, даже в Киев прорывались. И все из дому, все из дому. А приходит такой день, и голодный обратно к себе в хату заползает. Это значит: осилил голод, и человек уже не спасается, ложится на постель и лежит. И раз человека голод осилил, его не подымешь, и не только оттого, что сил нет – нет ему интереса, жить не хочется. Лежит себе тихо, и не тронь его. И есть голодному не хочется, мочится всё время и понос, и голодный становится сонный, не тронь его, только бы тихо было. Лежат голодные и доходят. Это рассказывали и военнопленные – если ложится пленный боец на нары, за пайкой не тянется, значит, конец ему скоро. А на некоторых безумие находило. Эти уж до конца не успокаивались. Их по глазам видно – блестят. Вот такие мёртвых разделывали и варили, и своих детей убивали и съедали. В этих зверь поднимался, когда человек в них умирал. Я одну женщину видела, в райцентр её привезли под конвоем – лицо человечье, а глаза волчьи. Их людоедов, говорили, расстреливали всех поголовно. А они не виноваты, виноваты те, что довели мать до того, что она своих детей ест. Да разве найдёшь виноватого – кого не спроси. Это ради хорошего, ради всех людей, матерей довели.

Я тогда увидела: всякий голодный – он, вроде, людоед. Мясо сам с себя объедает, одни кости остаются, жир до последней капельки. Потом он разумом темнеет – значит, и мозги свои съел. Съел голодный себя всего. Ещё я думала – каждый голодный по-своему умирает. В одной хате война идёт, друг за другом следят, друг у дружки крохи отнимают. Жена на мужа, муж против жены. Мать детей ненавидит. А в другой хате любовь нерушимая. Я знала одну такую, четверо детей, она сказки им рассказывает, чтобы про голод забыли, а у самой язык не

207

ворочается, она их на руки берёт, а у самой силы нет пустые руки поднять. А любовь в ней живёт. И замечали люди – где ненависть, там скорей умирали. Э, да что любовь, тоже никого не спасла, вся деревня поголовно легла. Не осталось жизни.

всё – всё время
райцентр – regional Party centre
голод – this grim extract from Grossman's last, grim novel is a fictionalised report of the terrible and unnecessary famine of 1932–3 which decimated the population of the Ukraine.

Considering the subject-matter, do you find the passage gains or loses by the reporter's tone?
How much do structure, language and syntax contribute to the impact of this extract?

Н. А. ЗАБОЛО́ЦКИЙ –
Лицо коня
(1926)

Животные не спят. Они во тьме ночной
Стоят над миром каменной стеной.

Рогами гладкими шумит в соломе
Покатая коровы голова.
Раздвинув скулы вековые,
Её притиснул каменистый лоб,
И вот косноязычные глаза
С трудом вращаются по кругу.

Лицо коня прекрасней и умней.
Он слышит говор листьев и камней.
Внимательный! Он знает крик звериный
И в ветхой роще рокот соловьиный.

И зная всё, кому расскажет он
Свои чудесные виденья?
Ночь глубока. На тёмный небосклон
Восходят звёзд соединенья.
И конь стоит, как рыцарь на часах,
Играет ветер в лёгких волосах,
Глаза горят, как два огромных мира,
И грива стелется, как царская порфира.

И если б человек увидел
Лицо волшебное коня,
Он вырвал бы язык бессильный свой
И отдал бы коню. Поистине достоин
Иметь язык волшебный конь!

Мы услыхали бы слова.
Слова большие, словно яблоки. Густые,
Как мёд или крутое молоко.

Слова, которые вонзаются, как пламя,
И, в душу залетев, как в хижину огонь,
Убогое убранство освещают.
Слова, которые не умирают
И о которых песни мы поём.

Но вот конюшня опустела,
Деревья тоже разошлись,
Скупое утро горы спеленало,
Поля открыло для работ.
И лошадь в клетке из оглобоь,
Повозку крытую влача,
Глядит покорными глазами
В таинственный и неподвижный мир.

What is the poet's attitude to his theme and how is this reflected in his use of diction and syntax?

How does the poem develop and what part does the uneven stanza structure play in the poem's development?

Comment on the effectiveness of the poem's imagery.

Comment on Zabolotsky's vocabulary and phraseology – are they striking? effective? appropriate?

To what extent does he exploit the interplay of rhyme, rhythm and metrical form?

М. ГÓРЬКИЙ –

Мои университеты

(1923)

Под Казанью села на камень, проломив днище, большая баржа с персидским товаром; артель грузчиков взяла меня перегружать баржу. Был сентябрь, дул верховый ветер, по серой реке сердито прыгали волны, ветер бешено срывая их гребни, кропил реку холодным дождём. Артель, человек полсотни, угрюмо расположилась на палубе пустой баржи, кутаясь рогожами и брезентом; баржу тащил маленький буксирный пароход, задыхаясь, выбрасывая в дождь красные снопы искр.

Вечерело. Свинцовое, мокрое небо, темнея, опускалось над рекою. Грузчики ворчали и ругались, проклиная дождь, ветер, жизнь, лениво ползли по палубе, пытаясь спрятаться от холода и сырости. Мне казалось, что эти полусонные люди не способны к работе, не спасут погибающий груз. К полуночи доплыли до переката, причалили пустую баржу борт о борт к сидевшей на камнях; артельный староста, ядовитый старичишка, рябой хитрец и сквернослов, с глазами и носом коршуна, сорвав с лысого черепа мокрый картуз, крикнул высоким, бабьим голосом:

– Молись, ребята!

В темноте, на палубе баржи, грузчики сбились в чёрную кучу и заворчали, как медведи, а староста, кончив молиться раньше всех, завизжал:

– Фонарей! Ну, молодчики, покажи работу! Честно, детки! С Богом – начинай!

И тяжёлые, ленивые, мокрые люди начали 'показывать работу'. Они, точно, в бой, бросились на палубу и в трюмы затонувшей баржи, – с гиком, рёвом, с прибаутиками. Вокруг меня с лёгкостью пуховых подушек летали мешки риса, тюки изюма, кож, каракуля, бегали коренастые фигуры, ободряя друг друга воем, свистом, крепкой руганью. Трудно было поверить, что так весело, легко и скоро работают те самые тяжёлые, угрюмые люди, которые только что уныло жаловались на жизнь, на дождь и холод. Дождь стал гуще, холоднее, ветер усилился, рвал рубахи, закидывая подолы на головы, обнажая животы. В мокрой тьме при свете шести фонарей метались чёрные люди, глухо топая ногами о палубы барж. Работали так, изголодались о труде, как будто давно ожидали удовольствия швырять с рук на руки четырёхпудовые мешки, бегом носиться с тюками на спине. Работали играя, с весёлым увлечением детей, с той пьяной радостью делать, слаще которой только объятие женщины.

Gor'ky is a better observer than interpreter: which is he in this extract?

Do tone, structure and contrast of images play any part in the passage's impact?

Are Gor'ky's vocabulary and phraseology at all striking, idiosyncratic or memorable?

How successfully does he convey the transformation in the artel'?

А. А. ВОЗНЕСЕ́НСКИЙ –
Антимиры

(1961)

Живёт у нас сосед Букашкин,
В кальсонах цвета промокашки.
Но, как воздушные шары,
Над ним горят

Антимиры!
И в них магический, как демон,
Вселенной правит, возлежит
Антибукашкин, академик,
И щупает Лоллобриджид.

Но грезятся Антибукашкину
Виденья цвета промокашки.

Да здравствуют Антимиры!
Фантасты – посреди муры.
Без глупых не было бы умных,
Оазисов – без Каракумов.

Нет женщин –

есть антимужчины.
В лесах ревут антимашины.
Есть соль земли. Есть сор земли.
Но сохнет сокол без змеи.

Люблю я критиков моих.
На шее одного из них,
Благоуханна и гола,
Сияет антиголова!...

... Я сплю с окошками открытыми,
А где-то свищет звездопад,
И небоскрёбы

сталактитами

213

На брюхе глобуса висят.

И подо мной
                    вниз головой,
Вонзившись вилкой в шар земной,
Беспечный, милый мотылёк,
Живёшь ты, мой антимирок!

Зачем среди ночной поры
Встречаются антимиры?

Зачем они вдвоём сидят
И в телевизоры глядят?

Им не понять и пары фраз.
Их первый раз – последний раз!

Сидят, забывши про бонтон,
Ведь будут мучиться потом!
И ушки красные горят,
Как будто бабочки сидят ...

... Знакомый лектор мне вчера
Сказал: 'Антимиры? Мура!'
Я сплю, ворочаюсь спросонок.
Наверно, прав научный хмырь ...

Мой кот, как радиоприёмник,
Зелёным глазом ловит мир.

Лоллобриджид – Gina Lollobrigida, a shapely Italian film-star.
Каракумов – the Kara-Kum desert of Turkmen S.S.R.
хмырь – хрыч

Having ascertained the nature of an *антимир*, show to what artistic use Voznesensky has put it in this poem and how, if at all, he develops his ideas. Compare his attitude to science, as implied by this poem, with Khlebnikov's (q.v.).

What is the tone of this poem and how is it signalled?

Voznesensky has been called one of the most original poets since the 'Thaw'. Consider his use of language, imagery, metre and rhyme and compare it with Yevtushenko's (q.v.).

Do you sense the influence of a major Russian poet of the early twentieth century and in what respects?

Е. И. ЗАМЯТИН –

Мы

(1920)

На первой странице Государственной газеты сияло:

'Радуйтесь,

Ибо отныне вы – совершенны! До сего дня ваши же детища, механизмы – были совершеннее вас.

Чем?

Каждая искра динамо – искра чистейшего разума, каждый ход поршня – непорочный силлогизм. Но разве не тот же безошибочный разум и в вас?

Философия у кранов, прессов и насосов – закончена и ясна, как циркульный круг. Но разве ваша философия менее циркульна?

Красота механизма – в неуклонном и точном, как маятник, ритме. Но разве вы, с детства вскормлённые системой Тейлора – не стали маятниково-точны?

И только одно:

У механизма нет фантазии.

Вы видели когда-нибудь, чтобы во время работы на физиономии у насосного цилиндра – расплывалась далёкая, бессмысленно-мечтательная улыбка? Вы слышали когда-нибудь, чтобы краны по ночам, в часы, назначенные для отдыха, беспокойно ворочались и вздыхали?

Нет!

А у вас – краснейте! – Хранители всё чаще видят эти улыбки и вздохи. И – прячьте глаза, – историки Единого Государства просят отставки, чтобы не записывать постыдных событий.

Но эта не ваша вина – вы больны. Имя этой болезни:

фантазия.

Это – червь, который выгрызает чёрные морщины на лбу. Это – лихорадка, которая гонит вас бежать всё дальше – хотя бы это 'дальше' начиналось там, где кончается счастье. Это – последняя баррикада на пути к счастью.

И радуйтесь: она уже взорвана.

Путь свободен.

Последнее открытие Государственной Науки: центр фантазии – жалкий мозговой узелок в области Варолиева моста.

Трёхкратное прижигание этого узелка X-лучами – и вы излечены от фантазии –

Навсегда.

Вы-совершенны, вы – машиноравны, путь к стопроцентному счастью – свободен. Спешите же все – стар и млад – спешите подвергнуться Великой Операции. Спешите в аудиториумы, где производится Великая Операция. Да здравствует Великая Операция! Да здравствует Единое Государство, да здравствует Благодетель!'

системой Тейлора – a reference to the American F. W. Taylor (1856–1915), the 'father of scientific management'.

Варолиева моста – the 'Pons Varolii', a part of the brain stem, supposedly discovered by the sixteenth-century Italian anatomist Costanzo Varolio.

This is an extract from a novel which decisively influenced Orwell's *1984*, yet is little known now both in and outside the Soviet Union. What momentous event is being described, and what is the tone of the announcement itself and the author's tone? Point to significant uses of diction and syntax in your answer.

How do the passage's structure and graphic layout contribute to its effectiveness?

Consider Zamyatin's vocabulary and phraseology – would you consider them striking and original, especially his inclusion of the vocabulary of twentieth-century technology?

Е. А. БОРАТЫ́НСКИЙ –
Бокал
(1835)

Полный влагой искрометной,
Зашипел ты, мой бокал!
И покрыл туман приветный
Твой озябнувший кристалл ...
Ты не встречен братьей шумной,
Буйных оргий властелин, –
Сластолюбец вольнодумный,
Я сегодня пью один.

Чем душа моя богата,
Всё твоё, о друг Аи!
Ныне мысль моя не сжата
И свободны сны мои;
За струёю вдохновенной
Не рассеян данник твой
Бестолково оживлённой,
Разногласною толпой.

Мой восторг неосторожный
Не обидит никого;
Не откроет дружбе ложной
Таин счастья моего;
Не смутит глупцов ревнивых
И торжественных невежд
Излияньем горделивых
Иль святых моих надежд!

Вот теперь со мной беседуй,
Своенравая струя!
Упоенья проповедуй
Иль отравы бытия;
Сердцу милые преданья

Благодатно оживи
Или прошлые страданья
Мне на память призови!

О бокал уединенья!
Не усилены тобой
Пошлой жизни впечатленья,
Словно чашей круговой;
Плодородней, благородней,
Дивной силой будишь ты
Откровенья преисподней
Иль небесные мечты.

И один я пью отныне!
Не в людском шуму пророк –
В немотствующей пустыне
Обретает свет высок!
Не в бесплодном развлеченьи
Общежительных страстей –
В одиноком упоеньи
Мгла падёт с его очей!

Au – a kind of champagne.

What elements in Boratynsky's style (e.g. tone, subject-matter, imagery, diction) are redolent of the eighteenth century? (c.f. Lermontov, Pushkin, Tyutchev and Derzhavin in making your choice.)

What do you consider distinctive about Boratynsky's style in this poem?

How would you describe the nature of his poetic thought? (c.f. Brodsky, Aliger and Pasternak in making your decision.)

М. А. БУЛГА́КОВ –
Белая гвардия
(1924)

Ещё в сентябре никто в Городе не представлял себе, что могут соорудить три человека, обладающие талантом появиться вовремя, даже и в таком ничтожном месте, как Белая Церковь. В октябре об этом уже сильно догадывались, и начали уходить, освещёнными сотнями огней, поезда с Города 1, Пассажирского, в новый, пока ещё широкий лаз через новоявленную Польшу и в Германию. Полетели телеграммы. Уехали бриллианты, бегающие глаза, проборы и деньги. Рвались и на юг, на юг, в приморский город Одессу. В ноябре месяце, увы! – все уже знали довольно определённо. Слово
    – Петлюра!
        – Петлюра!!
    – Петлюра! –
запрыгало со стен, с серых телеграфных сводок. Утром с газетных листков оно капало в кофе, и божественный тропический напиток немедленно превращался во рту в неприятнейшие помои. Оно загуляло по языкам и застучало в аппаратах Морзе у телеграфистов под пальцами. В Городе начались чудеса в связи с этим же загадочным словом, которое немцы произносили по-своему:
    – Пэтурра.
Отдельные немецкие солдаты, приобревшие скверную привычку шататься по окраинам, начали по ночам исчезать. Ночью исчезали, а днём выяснилось, что их убивали. Поэтому заходили по ночам немецкие патрули в цирюльных тазах. Они ходили, и фонарики сияли – не безобразничать! Но никакие фонарики не могли рассеять той мутной каши, которая заварилась в головах.

Вильгельм. Вильгельм. Вчера убили трёх немцев. Боже, немцы уходят, вы знаете?! Троцкого арестовали рабочие в Москве!! Сукины сыны какие-то остановили поезд под Бородянкой и начисто его ограбили. Петлюра послал посольство в Париж. Опять Вильгельм. Чёрные сингалезы в Одессе. Неизвестное, таинственное имя – консул Энно. Одесса. Одесса. Генерал Деникин. Опять Вильгельм. Немцы уйдут, французы придут.

– Большевики придут, батенька!

– Типун тебе на язык, батюшка!

У немцев есть такой аппарат со стрелкой – поставят его на землю, и стрелка показывает, где оружие зарыто. Это штука. Петлюра послал посольство к большевикам. Это ещё лучше штука. Петлюра. Петлюра. Петлюра. Петлюра. Пэтурра.

Город – Kiev in 1918 (Why should Bulgakov refer to it as such?)

три человека – the leaders of the Ukrainian nationalist movement after the February revolution of 1917. They were Hrushevsky, a history professor; Vinnichenko, a revolutionary intellectual, and Petlyura (q.v. infra).

Белая Церковь – a small town about 50km south of Kiev.

новоявленную Польшу – Poland had now become an independent republic.

Одесса – a major port on the Black Sea, used during the Civil War as an escape route to the West.

Петлюра – after a brief spell as the Secretary for Military Affairs in the Ukrainian Rada (the name given to the post-February nationalist government) from March 1917 to February 1918, Simon Petlyura created an extreme nationalist movement which, trained with French assistance, was ready to march on Kiev by autumn 1918. Petlyura's Ukrainian peasant army was chiefly remembered for its lawless savagery and anti-Semitism.

в цирюльных тазах – the nickname for the German military helmets.

Вильгельм – Kaiser Wilhelm II abdicated and escaped to Holland in November 1918.

Троцкого – Trotsky, the Bolshevik People's Commissar for Foreign Affairs until the Treaty of Brest-Litovsk in March 1918, after which he became Commissar for War.

Бородянкой – Borodyanka, a small town on the north-west edge of Kiev.

сингалезы – part of the French Intervention Forces in Odessa.

Генерал Деникин – General Anton Denikin became Supreme Commander of the White Forces in March 1918.

In this extract from his novel, *The White Guard*, how does Bulgakov report events in Kiev in late 1918, and how does his reporting differ from a scholarly 'history' of the same events? What is the effect of the subtle irony pervading the passage? How does the structure of the passage increase its effectiveness?

What is the effect of the repetition of certain names, places and events?

To what extent does Bulgakov exploit rhythmic diversity?

What is the effect of the personification of inanimate objects?

А. А. ЗИНÓВЬЕВ –

Зияющие высоты

(1976)

'Страничка героической истории'

Во времена Хозяина был установлен единый общеибанский стандарт штанов. Один тип штанов на все возрасты и росты. На все полности и должности. Широкие в поясе, в коленках и внизу. С мотнёй до колен. С чётко обозначенной ширинкой и карманами до пят. Идеологически выдержанные штаны. По этим штанам ибанцев безошибочно узнавали во всём мире. И сейчас ещё на улицах Ибанска можно иногда увидеть эти живые памятники славной эпохи Хозяина. Их демонстративно донашивают пенсионеры-соратники Хозяина. Донашивают ли? Однажды Журналист спросил обладателя таких штанов, как он ухитрился их сохранить до сих пор. Пенсионер потребовал предъявить документ. Потом сказал, что он эти штаны сшил совсем недавно. Когда Журналист уходил, пенсионер прошипел ему вслед: распустились, мерзавцы, к стенке давно вас не ставили. Это, конечно, смешной курьёз. К стенке можно ставить и в узких штанах и даже без штанов. Даже удобнее.

Выработан всеибанский тип штанов был в ожесточённой борьбе с уклонами и классовыми врагами. Левые уклонисты хотели сделать штаны шире в поясе, а мотню спереди опустить до пят. Они рассчитывали построить полный изм в ближайшие полгода и накормить изголодавшихся трудящихся до отвала. Своевременно выступил Хозяин и поправил их. Лэвые укланысты, сказал он, савершыли тыпычную ашыпку. Аны атарвалыс ат масс и забыжалы впэрод. Левых уклонистов ликвидировали правые уклонисты. Те, напротив, хотели расширить штаны в коленках и ликвидировать ширинку. Они не верили в творческие потенции масс и все надежды возложили на буржуазию. Опять своевременно выступил Хозяин и поправил их. Правыэ укланысты, сказал он, савэршылы тыпычную ашыпку. Аны атарвалыс ат масс и забыжалы назат. Правых уклонистов

221

ликвидировали левые.

Когда Хозяин сдох и ибанцы наревелись досыта, стали появляться несколько зауженные штаны. Потом появились совсем узкие. С узкоштанниками повели решительную борьбу. Разрезали штаны публично, выгоняли из институтов, увольняли с работы, штрафовали, писали фельетоны. Но зато уже не расстреливали. И расправу производили не Органы, а сами широкие народные массы по собственному почину. Страшили не узкие штаны сами по себе. Они были даже выгоднее, так как благодаря им производство тканей в стране выросло сразу вдвое. Узкие штаны были признаком и символом растущей непокорности, своеволия, неверия. Но в конце концов узкие штаны, как и кибернетика, были очищены от идеологических искажений и признаны отвечающими идеалам изма. Как раз к этому времени они устарели.

Хозяин – the leader of the imaginary town of Ibansk, and also the nickname applied to Stalin. Ibansk itself is probably a pun on a well-known Russian obscenity.

мотня – a piece of extra material sewn into a pair of trousers where the legs begin.

Журналист – a fictional amalgam of Western correspondents.

борьба с уклонами – Stalin's rise to supreme power involved long intra-Party struggles with the so-called 'Left Opposition', led by Trotsky, and the so-called 'Right Opposition', led by Bukharin, both of which were ultimately physically liquidated.

изм – a reference to the Soviet political practice of labelling any supposedly deviant form of political activity an '-ism'.

Лэвые ... впэрод and *Правыэ ... назат* – a parody of Stalin's Georgian accent.

Органы – the security organs or 'secret police'.

Study carefully in this extract Zinov'ev's subject-matter (do you see in it echoes of Soviet political history?), structure, tone and all aspects of style, and consider the statement that 'Zinov'ev's prose style is an idiosyncratic mixture of Swift, Zamyatin and Soviet political jargon', referring for elucidation to the extract from *Мы*, the study of Soviet political prose and Swift's *Modest Proposal*.

М. Е. САЛТЫКО́В-ЩЕДРИ́Н –
Господа Головлёвы
(1876)

Сегодняшний штоф привёл за собой целый последовательный ряд новых, и с этих пор он аккуратно каждую ночь напивался. В девять часов, когда в конторе гасил свет и люди расходились по своим логовищам, он ставил на стол припасённый штоф с водкой и ломоть чёрного хлеба, густо посыпанный солью. Не сразу он приступал к водке, а словно подкрадывался к ней. Кругом всё засыпало мёртвым сном; только мыши скреблись за отставшими от стен обоями да часы назойливо тикали в конторе. Снявши халат, в одной рубашке, сновал он взад и вперёд по жарко натопленной комнате, по временам останавливался, подходил к столу, нашаривал в темноте штоф и вновь принимался за ходьбу. Первые рюмки он выпивал с прибаутками, сладострастно всасывая в себя жгучую влагу; но мало-помалу биение сердца учащалось, голова загоралась – и язык начинал бормотать что-то несвязное. Притупленное воображение силилось создать какие-то образы, помертвелая память пробовала в область прошлого, но образы выходили разорванные, бессмысленные, а прошлое не откликалось ни единым воспоминанием, ни горьким, ни светлым, словно между ним и настоящей минутой раз навсегда встала плотная стена. Перед ним было только настоящее в форме наглухо запертой тюрьмы, в которой бесследно потонула и идея пространства, и идея времени. Комната, печь, три окна в наружной стене, деревянная скрипучая кровать и на ней тонкий, притоптанный тюфяк, стол с стоящим на нём штофом – ни до каких других горизонтов мысль не додумывалась. Но, по мере того как убывало содержание штофа, по мере того как голова распалялась, – даже и это скудное чувство настоящего становилось не под силу. Бормотанье, имевшее вначале хоть какую-нибудь форму, окончательно разлагалось; зрачки глаз, усиливаясь различить очертания тьмы, безмерно расширялись; самая тьма, наконец, исчезала, и взамен её являлось пространство, наполненное фосфорическим блеском. Это была бесконечная пустота, мёртвая, не откликающаяся ни единым жизненным звуком, зловеще-лучезарная. Она следовала за ним по пятам, за каждым оборотом его шагов. Ни стен, ни окон, ничего не существовало; одна безгранично тянущаяся, светящаяся пустота. Ему становилось страшно; ему нужно было заморить в себе чувство действительности до такой степени, чтобы даже пустоты не было. Ещё несколько усилий – и он был у цели. Спотыкающиеся ноги из стороны в сторону носили онемевшее тело, грудь издавала не бормотанье, а хрип, самое существование как бы прекращалось. Наступало то странное оцепенение, которое, нося на себе все признаки сознательной жизни, вместе с тем несомненно указывала на присутствие какой-то особенной жизни, развивавшейся независимо от каких-то ни было условий. Стоны за стонами вырывались из груди, нимало не нарушая сна; органический недуг продолжал свою разъедающую работу, не причиняя, по-видимому, физических болей.

This is a typical extract from what has been called 'one of the gloomiest novels in all Russian literature'. Consider all the elements (development, tone, diction, syntax, rhythm) which contribute to its astonishing impact.

GLOSSARY AND INDEX OF UNFAMILIAR TERMS

Accentual metre: in accentual metre only the number of stresses per line is taken into account, while the number of unstressed syllables, between the stresses, is variable. The concept of the 'foot' has no place in accentual metre. 21, 103

Anapaest: a foot consisting of two short (or unstressed) syllables followed by one long (or stressed) syllable. Meaning 'reversed' in Greek, this foot is a 'reversed' dactyl (q.v.). 41, 52, 92, 115

Anaphora: the repetition of a word or phrase for aesthetic effect. 98, 138

Apostrophe: an exclamatory address to a particular person or thing. 29, 30, 51, 52

Caesura: a pause in a line of verse at a particular place, the latter depending on the prosodic tradition. 7, 21, 22, 30, 31, 40, 66, 67, 80, 81, 84, 138

Chiasmus: inversion in the second phrase of the order followed in the first, e.g. *люди, обсыпанные вшами, как этими людьми теплушки* (Пильняк). 66, 86, 87, 130

Dactyl: a foot consisting of a long (or stressed) syllable followed by two short (or unstressed) ones. Meaning 'finger' in Greek, this foot resembles the relative bone lengths in the index-fingers. 30, 64, 73, 105

Dactylic rhyme: a form of rhyme where the stress falls on the antepenultimate syllable e.g. *стрáнники/изгнáнники* (Лермонтов). 41, 114

Dimeter: a line of verse consisting of two metric feet. 124

End-stopping: a compulsory pause for effect at the end of a line by a punctuational device. 21, 30, 40, 52, 53, 64, 66, 67, 94, 103, 105, 124, 137, 138

Enjambement (French): the continuation of a sentence or clause beyond the confines of a single line of verse into a subsequent one.   21, 30, 65, 66, 81, 138

Feminine rhyme: a form of rhyme where the stress falls on the penultimate syllable, e.g. *другою/береговою* (Цветаева).
6, 52, 64, 80, 114, 124

Heroic: as in 'heroic couplet' – in English verse a couplet in iambic pentameter rhyming *aabb* etc., has been, since Chaucer, statistically the most common prosodic form. 20

Homeric simile: an extended simile in which the vehicle may be a whole scene rather than a single object, e.g. the final six lines in the excerpt from 'Повесть о том, как Иван Иванович поссорился с Иваном Никифоровичем' (Гоголь).   6, 13, 14

Hypotaxis: the linking of sentence elements by co-ordination and subordination to form a complex, extended whole, e.g. the sentence in the excerpt from *Anna Karenina* beginning, 'Если и была причина ...'   27, 58, 130

Iambus: a metrical foot consisting of one short (or unstressed) syllable followed by one long (or stressed) syllable; apparently so called because of its suggesting (to the Greeks) a limp.   6, 20, 52, 92, 124, 137, 139

Masculine rhyme: a form of rhyme where the stress falls on the final syllable, e.g. *острова/Москва* (Пушкин).
52, 64, 80, 103, 114, 124

Parallelism: a rhythmical device whereby successive phrases, clauses or sentences are compared or made to correspond, e.g. in *Anna Karenina* – 'Либеральная партия говорила, что брак ...'.   26, 27, 30, 46, 59, 72, 73, 88, 99, 100, 105, 109, 110, 119, 120, 130, 131, 132, 144, 145

Parataxis: the placing of sentence elements one after the other, without words to indicate co-ordination or subordination, e.g. 'Он скрипел, шуршал, потрескивал, вздрагивал ...' (Казаков) or 'Veni, vidi, vici!'   26, 27, 59, 60, 72, 73, 74, 75, 87, 88, 98, 108, 109, 110, 119, 120, 130, 131, 132, 144, 149

Periphrasis: a roundabout way of speaking, a circumlocution, e.g. 'Печальный пасынок природы' (Пушкин).   7, 36, 82

Rejet (French): a word (or words) carried over into a subsequent line by enjambement (q.v.) and enhanced thereby.
30, 66, 81

Spondee: a metrical foot consisting of two long (or stressed) syllables.   105

Stump-compound: a form of abbreviation which, though used to a limited extent before 1917, has created at least 20,000 new forms since then, e.g. *политрук* < *политический руководитель; Южуралмашзавод* < *южноуральский машинный завод.*   109, 144

Synaesthesia: a deliberate and apparently paradoxical 'mixing of the senses' for effect, e.g. '*Запахов было множество, и все они звучали* ...' (Казаков).   74, 105, 110, 131

Synecdoche: a rhetorical device wherein a part stands for the whole, e.g. '*глядел ... лицом*' (Белый).   73

Tenor: the object of a comparison.   99

Tetrameter: a line of verse consisting of four metric feet.
                                        6, 20, 30, 124

Trochee: a metrical foot consisting of one long (or stressed) syllable followed by one short (or unstressed) syllable. Meaning a 'running foot', it resembles the respective emphasis on the feet used in running.   80, 104

Truncated rhyme: a form of rhyme used by some poets since about 1920, whereby only identity of the stressed vowel is necessary, e.g. *кроясь/поезд* (Есенин).   80, 103, 114, 124